Find Your
DESTINY

TEN SIMPLE APPROACHES TO SUCCESSFUL
ENTREPRENEURSHIP AND HAPPINESS

MOY TEO

PARTRIDGE

Library of Congress Control Number:		2020908190
ISBN:	Hardcover	978-1-5437-5820-7
	Softcover	978-1-5437-5819-1
	eBook	978-1-5437-5821-4

To order additional copies of this book, contact
Toll Free 800 101 2657 (Singapore)
Toll Free 1 800 81 7340 (Malaysia)
orders.singapore@partridgepublishing.com

www.partridgepublishing.com/singapore

CONTENTS

WHY I DECIDED to write this book, and where does the inspiration come from? Every person must always start with the question why in whatever new endeavor that they want to attempt. Most people lead their life in a routine fashion without asking this question, thereby walking a path that led to nowhere and regrets. Asking why saves you precious time of walking a journey that is already wrong from the beginning. As the entrepreneur path is a challenging route that either makes or breaks you, you have to be fully well prepared in all aspects before you start this journey that eventually only a minority few can make it.

Since young, being brought up in a very poor family background, I always fantasized about how it would look like to be successful and rich one day. Both my parents are illiterate, with my dad being a laborer and my mum being a general cleaner. They needed to feed a family of eight (my grandma and five kids, myself being the youngest) to make ends meet, and all of us squeezed into a very small one-room apartment, all sleeping on the floor with unrolled straw mats. Life was hard, but we got by. I can still remember that we used to have a biscuit tin from which we would share the bits and pieces of biscuits among us. Food such as chicken was indeed a luxury for our indulgence during that time. Lunar New Year used to be our favorite period, as this was the only time when we could enjoy some real delicacies and get our small red packets from our parents and relatives.

Looking back almost forty years, I could see how my life seems to be like a roller-coaster ride with so many ups and downs. However, it is always during the down zone that my inner driver and state of mind is challenged to push past the limits, to break through to the next level. Thinking back, I am so grateful for these downside experiences that molded me to be what I am today. *Tough times create tough people and impart us with experiences that are irreplaceable. Knowledge is power, but knowledge plus experience through consistent positive actions is the ultimate invincible power that makes all great people achieve whatever they want in their lives.*

From a pauper to decamillionaire (any person with a net worth of 10 million and above in USD, euro, or pounds sterling)? A lot of people are curious about how many entrepreneurs achieve this level from very humble backgrounds, with not a single cent in their pocket. This is what inspires me deeply to share our journey with the hope that our younger generations and those who read this book will be motivated to have the courage to believe in their dreams and take on the challenging entrepreneur path. Regardless of age, you can still pursue your dreams and what you believe in. (Never forget the classic story of KFC and how Colonel Sanders started promoting his grandma's fried chicken recipe door-to-door at the age of sixty-five and become a billionaire at the age of eighty-eight) Attitude is all that matters. Where there is a will, there is always a way in life. If there is ever one such person in this world who had done something before, there is no reason why you cannot achieve the same.

Another big motivating factor that triggers my inner fire and drive to write this book is my deep sense of gratitude and appreciation toward all the people who have walked through this thrilling journey with me. Not only do I thank all those kind souls who had believed in me as a simple, humble person to be able to make my goals come true, I am also equally grateful to those individuals who are skeptical about my vision. I always keep an open mind and will take all comments on board with a positive mindset of seeking improvement. We cannot control what others think and feel or do to us, but we definitely can control our own mind on how we perceive and interpret such actions and how to always apply positivity and handle such situations in an amicable and calm manner. As China's legendary and historic wise figure Laozi (founder of Daoism and believed to be the author of the Tao-te Ching) preaches, "Live in harmony with the world and follow the flow of life by balancing our Yin/Yang and all good will eventually come to you."

No one can really be self-made to be successful in whatever goal they had set themselves into. As an entrepreneur, whatever business you choose to be in, you need to create or build something that can add value to other people. Why are companies like Apple, Microsoft, Amazon, and Facebook so successful? Simply by creating a product or service whereby other people find a need or connection in what they are marketing and selling. It sounds so simple, and yet in reality, it is not easy to achieve. The key to success involves the support and connection from other people. Therefore, do not confuse being self-reliant with being self-made; the former gives you absolute power to be in control of your destiny, whereas the latter is just illusionary and egoistic. Being self-reliant means you assume full responsibility, embrace full accountability, and lead by examples. By being fully informed—doing detailed research and analysis—and applying these data from the aspect of practicality, a person can then master the art of self-reliance.

As I take you all along to share some entrepreneur philosophy and experience that I had compiled, the greatest joy in writing this book is sharing the interesting characters of those business associates who had walked this path side by side with me and sharing their own motivational success stories that can be so inspiring and educational. Words cannot express my gratitude to all these close affiliates and alliances who had supported me along this challenging journey. It is often the experience and lessons learned during our journey and not the final destiny that make our life meaningful and what really enlighten and develop us into wiser people. Without them coming into my life at different stages of this journey, especially in times of need and crisis, I do not think I will be able to make it as a humble individual.

What profession did I choose in my career that led to my small success? I am not a smart or fast learner. (I only started talking at age of four and was very slow to acquire basic motor and cognitive skills as a young kid.) I am not inclined to technology, nor am I good with social media. I only have one survival skill, and that is in the art of selling. Since youth, I have always tried to sell almost anything I could get hold of to transform them to some monetary value. I would buy an eraser from a friend in my school for ten cents and sell this same eraser to my neighbor for twenty cents. Thinking back, I feel grateful to be born in a family that was not well-to-do; poverty, if taken from a positive perspective, does have a positive impact that will be beneficial to us this lifetime. The desire to improve one's current conditions and be out of poverty can be so empowering that it can basically transform a person's survival instinct into unlimited power and will to strive for ultimate success. With such mindset and daily practice since young, I am subconsciously trained to polish my interpersonal skills to become a top salesperson, swearing an oath to turn this into my lifelong profession. After grinding and hustling for many years, doing my own trading business as a local owner handling suppliers, employees and customers from the top to the bottom levels, I finally reached the finish line of this journey and sold my business to a listed group in the Netherlands. Moving forward, I am taking my career path to the next horizon by assisting them to build a bigger platform within APAC, outside my circle of Singaporean and Malaysian influence.

Simultaneously, I would like to do more for our society, thereby writing this book and sharing inspirational speeches to all people who have a passion in choosing sales as their lifelong profession. I would also like to build a deeper connection with individuals who would like to lead a happier and more successful life by helping them with goal-setting and setting parameters for their life priorities and objectives. With my own experience in a sales role for so many years, all I can comment is that sales is one of the few professions that can turn a pauper like myself into a millionaire in a very short time frame if we approach all our customers with the right attitude, integrity, and mindset. Sales is the only profession that can allow an individual to earn money with the minimum resource and investment cost. (A salesperson who attains mastery can easily sell shoes in Africa or ice in Alaska.) You do not need to have money in your pocket to make a fortune if you are smart in doing so. *All you need is your burning desire to believe in what you are selling and to share your enthusiasm to the end users, who benefit in turn from what you are sharing.* This is the simple fundamental principle of selling. Sales is all about communication, connection, negotiation, and finally, closing the deal with a big smile and handshake to strike win–win for all parties. The sky is always the limit for all top salespersons. They simply cannot thrive without daily challenges, for they fully understand that in such a competitive world, the moment they stop seeking improvement will be the day they will be overtaken by their immediate competitors. To be top in any profession, we must be able to adapt to constant changes and handle pressure, perceiving them as fun and enticing rather than turning them into stress and problems. Opportunities in the sales profession are always in abundance, and one of the key factors that differentiate the rich and successful from the average and poor is their ability to think in abundance. In order to have abundance in life, our mind must be able to perceive abundance and imagine that we already are in the state of abundance (law of attraction). The positive and unbeatable mindset for all top sales persons will always be that the best has yet to come, and we can always sell more despite whatever situations or circumstances we are in.

Success is by large no accident. Living a great life will not come merely by luck or chance. It will not fall from the sky, there is no magic wand, and sorry to say, there is also no quick fix. Learn from those successful people revolving around you, and preferably, get a mentor or mentors who can impart their valuable experiences to you. This will shorten your path to reach the level of success and happiness you are after.

There is no such thing as failure unless you fail to learn a lesson from what you had experienced. Successful people face failures more than others, which is why they can finally succeed in whatever vision they believe in and whatever goals that they set their mind on. Everyone will fail at some point of their life journey, but the most important attitude when such incidents do happen is to do deep soul-searching within yourself, understand why you fail, and learn from this episode to become a better and stronger person tomorrow. *As what Abraham Lincoln, the American president during the Civil War, said, "My great concern is not whether you have failed, but whether you are content with your failure."* Life is like running a marathon—we all run at our own pace. But eventually we will all get there, so just set our mind and soul to finish it.

Along the way, we should give others a helping hand if we can so that our own journey will be full of amazing colors, joy, and fulfillment when we reach the finish line (refer to chapter 1).

In sales, patience is silent power anticipating success. Do not expect to get the order as if customers owe you a living, but practice humility to earn it. Work hard, work fast, and work smart. Apply the 10X rules to amplify your sales target so that you can achieve big results while putting in the same amount of time and effort. Be ruthless and ferocious when it is the right time to attack but be subtle and observant when it is time to retreat. *As the legendary sales master Dale Carnegie (who is also the famous writer of the book* How to Win Friends and Influence People) *said, "When dealing with people, remember you are not dealing with creatures of logic, but with creatures bristling with prejudice and motivated by pride and vanity'."* Therefore, never impose or force our own logic upon our customers. Practice compassion and empathy, and always put yourselves in customers' perspective to look at things so that you can find common ground and solutions to close any difficult deal on hand (refer to chapter 2).

No one will believe you until you believe in yourself that you are living a life that is filled with integrity and consciousness. If you want people to support you, always live by example. If you want people to respect you, respect yourself and practice what is right and good for the mankind. Progression and growth lead to belief, so never stop learning. Feed yourself with self-development materials, new knowledge, and empowering thoughts; start taking real positive actions. Always begin with an end in mind and treasure the shortness of life. *As the great Greek stoic philosopher Seneca said, "It is not that we have a short space of time, but that we waste too much of it. Life is long enough, and it has been given in sufficiently generous measure to allow the accomplishment of the very greatest thing if the whole of it well invested."* Time and tide wait for no man, and money cannot buy time which is the most valuable asset of our precious life (refer to chapter 3).

Habits make or break you, so make use of the power of developing good habits. A habit is formed by consistent application and deep focus. Make it important, and for it to be hardwired inside you, plan and execute it until it becomes a steadfast habit that you will auto mode on a daily basis. *As the legendary Chinese kung fu actor-cum-director Bruce Lee says, "I fear not the man who has practiced 10000 kicks, but I do fear the man who has practiced one kick 10000 times."* Understand that the cycle of habit lies fundamentally in the four basic stages, namely cue (a signal that prompts an event or action), cravings (motivational force behind every habit), response (actual habit you perform in terms of thought or action), and reward (end result that satisfies or teaches us). Once you understand the fundamentals of habit forming, you will be able to derive a plan accordingly to these four stages of the cycle and get your handsome reward by the end of it (refer to chapter 4).

There is nothing you cannot have or achieve in life if you are willing to work for it and learn to say no to things that will not help you to reach your goal. Do understand that not everyone will be happy for your success. Some will be jealous, and some will be resentful. Those who truly support and love you will always be by your side and respect your standpoint on why you decide to go after what you want to focus on and to neglect the rest of the irrelevant matters. *As American founding father and polymath Benjamin Franklin said, "You may delay time but time will not."* This simple yet profound and deep-meaning sentence highlights the importance of valuing time and focusing on what is truly the most important in your life. If you are unable to reject other people, chances are that you will not be able to resist temptation yourself on what you are not supposed to splurge on that will make you drift away from your final destiny. Without clear, distinctive direction, you will end up in the wrong finish line. Successful people know where they are going right from the beginning (refer to chapter 5).

There are no reasonable limits relating to what you can achieve other than those that exist in your mind. Learn to visualize and think big to achieve greatness. What you can be is up to you; what you can do is up to you. You are your only limit. Do not ever let any toxic people around convince you otherwise, and build alliances with people that are better than you and believe in you. Nothing worthwhile in life comes easy. If it is worth the prize, it is worth the fight, so start today by having big dreams and big visions so that you can live a big life. *As what the founder of Apple, Steve Jobs, said, "Stay hungry, stay foolish."* All big ideas might seem stupid and impossible to many when you share, but it is totally OK. It is better to be stupid for what you want to build than to be clever on something that is not original and mediocre (refer to chapter 6).

Let go of the past, focus on the now, and plan for your future with complete mindfulness and wisdom. Be grateful of what you have in your life. Grateful people are successful and happy people. When you are grateful of whatever you have in your life, your life becomes better. Writing down and thinking about what you are grateful for every morning will transform your life. The very act of gratefulness will lead to a better mood and clearer mind, and lead to better results and naturally attract more positive outcome into our life. *As what American philosopher and famous writer of "Self-Reliance", Ralph Waldo Emerson, said, "Cultivate the habit of being grateful for every good thing that comes to you, and to give thanks continuously. And because all things have contributed to your advancement, you should include all things in your gratitude"* (refer to chapter 7.)

Never stop learning, and seek continuous improvement. The key to a great life is growth that comes from self-development. Knowing you are a self-nurtured person living a great life and setting good examples for people around you is life-transforming. *As what Winston Churchill, British politician and famous writer, said, "Continuous effort —not strength or intelligence is the key to unlock your potential."* Self-reliance is the greatest strength in life. People can rob you of all material possessions, but no one can take away your knowledge, experience, dignity, and wisdom in life. Live your life like a walking encyclopedia and not like an empty vessel that only makes noises that are nonconstructive and of no value (refer to chapter 8).

Live with integrity. With integrity, you have nothing to fear because you have nothing to hide. With integrity, you will do the right thing, so you will always be proud of what you are doing every day and be able to sleep well every night. Give your all and bear full responsibility. Nothing great in life comes to those who give less than everything. Success should never feel like a chore but a long-term passion that keeps you enthusiastic and always voluntarily doing more than you are paid for. It is never too late to be great, so take full responsibility of your life, and see the rewards you reap by doing this noble act that few people can fully achieve in life. *As what Holocaust survivor and famous writer of the book* A Man's Search for Meaning *Viktor Frankl said, "Ultimately man should not ask what the meaning of his life is, but rather must recognize that it is he who is asked. In a word, each man is questioned by life, and he can only answer to life by answering for his own life; to life he can only respond by being responsible"* (refer to chapter 9).

You can change the way you feel by changing the way you think and what you focus on. Never chase after money, but follow your purpose instead. Chase the purpose, and money will automatically come to you. Understand that money is the final reward, and this can only come with daily habits of doing what is right for yourself and for your business. The end result of financial freedom will be worth the sacrifice. *As what American magnate and investor Warren Buffet said,*

"Opportunities come infrequently. When it rains gold, put out the bucket, not the thimble. Be fearful when others are greedy and be greedy when others are fearful." Learn to take calculated risks in life when opportunities arise. Constantly practice delayed gratification, and always live below your means so that you can put money to good use and build your wealth to achieve financial freedom (refer to chapter 10).

THE PATH TOWARD ENTREPRENEURSHIP

CHAPTER 1

The Beauty of Failure and How to Conquer Fear of Failure and Benefit from It

ALL OF YOU must be wondering. This book is about *success*, so why am I sharing about the big topic of failure right from the beginning?

If you were to interview one hundred entrepreneurs who had made it in business about failure, all will agree that they failed more than any normal individuals before they made success happen. Failure is not an issue, but how you handle failure, learn from failure, and become a wiser person afterward is what really matters.

Most people do not fulfill their dreams because the moment they encounter setbacks, their mental, emotional, and psychological response to this bad experience will automatically prompt them to retreat and back off. To become a great entrepreneur, you have to get comfortable with or even appreciate failure, because this is where our comfortable adaption point is being challenged, and we are forced to push ourselves to the next limit. Constant practice and consistent habits of doing something to the extent of achieving mastery are what enable you to conquer failure at all times. Every great invention in this world exists because the creator experienced what does not work many times and kept doing the same actions over and over again until they got it right. Thomas Edison, the great inventor who had a hearing impairment since young, innovated 1,300 products during his lifetime, failed countless times before he succeeded to ignite his first light bulb, which glowed for only a mere forty seconds. (Just imagine our life in complete darkness at night without this invention!) *Fail early, fail often, fail forward,* and you will finally attain great success in the field that you want to excel in.

Statistics showed that only 1 percent of people really make it to the top in everything that they do to attain what we term as mastery. Are there anyone in the 99 percent of people around you who is not in this 1 percent? I presume there will be many. Being scared to fail will drive you further away from this 1 percent goal. Failure is never permanent. In fact, nothing in life is permanent, so the smartest way to overcome fear is to understand that all failure shall pass and you just have to keep trying until you get it right one fine day. Do not be worried about failure. Understand that everyone experience failure during some stages of our life, and that is one of the key principles to set us up for success later. Fear, just like many negative emotions, is simply an illusion. Fear has no life outside our imagination. Fear is mind-made and not real. The reason you are so afraid of it is due to the feeling of uncertainty. Knowing this, you have no reason to fear failure, rejection, or anything that can hinder your success. Believe in yourself, and go for whatever you deem is right to pursue. Discard fear, and you will discover abundant courage to pursue your big dream and big vision.

My first big failure in business was at the age of twenty-three, after going into a partnership with my best friend after our tertiary education. We both graduated from the University of Reading, majoring in food technology. With my burning desire to walk the path toward entrepreneurship, I invited her to join my venture into this health food trading business immediately after we came back from the UK. During year 1999, I saw the opportunity to bring in a range of organic heath food from the UK and Europe and set up this small trading company with her in Singapore. Despite the fact that I was honored to win the Young Scientist Award in the whole of UK for food faculty, with heaps of opportunities to work for big listed companies, I followed my heart and choose a different path from most of my peers. Most of them chose the career paths to work for others, mostly in R&D and laboratory positions, whereas I selected entrepreneurship to thrive on my own. As I did not have any money after graduation, the capital pumped in to set up this trading company came solely from my best friend's family. As I treasured this opportunity so dearly at that time of my life, I practically put my heart and soul into this small business that I envisioned to become a multimillion-dollar company. With the passion and creativity streaming in my blood, I focused on strategizing for the business and doing daily hustling groundwork to start growing our customer portfolio.

Our first breakthrough was when we managed to secure the distribution rights to Nature's Farm, one of the largest health food chains at that time. I will never forget the nice memories of giving health talks as one of the chosen speakers during Nature's Farm in-house seminars to their subscribed members. At age twenty-three, I was always the youngest speaker, and just imagine having to present in front of hundreds of audiences who themselves are mostly health experts from sound professions in medical, legal, banking, and other professions. Self-confidence is all that matters in life sometimes, and I was always praised for being the most bubbly, energetic, entertaining, and persuasive speaker at the end of each seminar. As I was well-liked by all the older uncles and aunties who had deep pockets for spending, this automatically acted as a booster in establishing a good relationship with Nature's Farm, thereby getting our business into smooth sailing in merely less than one year of our establishment. The best salesperson in the world will always be someone who radiates positive energy to those whom she wants to influence with absolute belief that she is adding value in whatever she is selling.

After our company started to build awareness and gain recognition within the local health food industry, things suddenly took a turn. I was asked by my best-friend-cum-partner to withdraw from the partnership, as I did not pump in any capital to start the company. I was not obliged to do so from a business perspective, as under the law, I was entitled 50 percent of the company. However, after much consideration, I still voluntarily withdrew my rightful share; maybe at the time, I was too hurt and disappointed to fight for a cause. I always treasure sentimental value more than monetary value, so maybe the emotional pain inflicted at that point of my life surpassed my desire from the practical monetary perspective. This was a hard lesson for me from both business and personal experience, as I really did put my heart and soul into the business with no salary drawn during this period—just with the will and determination to build our dream and passion together. I was heartbroken and was in a depressed mood for a while, even thinking suicidal thoughts at times.

It will take any person great willpower to walk out from any failed business venture, as you will suddenly feel complete emptiness from losing your career, finances, relationship, and social identity. You will feel like you are in a bottomless pit that is completely pitch-black, with no clue on how to move on as you cannot visualize any hope ahead. Both your mind and heart will keep demotivating you to let go and give up all hopes and dreams. You will suddenly find yourself losing all the will to go on and wanting to just leave it to fate to bring you wherever you are destined to land on. You will also not be at all motivated to do anything that involves any physical and cognitive effort. Simple daily tasks such as getting out of bed and brushing your teeth become chores, and you are like one aimless soul floating around in this universe. All you want to do is to be cut off from the outside world and to live in denial in your enclosed shallow dark space. At this point of life, moral support from your loved ones are super important, and some individuals might also seek professional psychiatrist help. As I was, at that time, so poor even to buy food to survive, I actually walked through this dark tunnel just through sheer willpower and endurance. As what people said, which I totally agree on, time is the best medicine. Wounds will just heal by themselves if you practice patience and faith, and let nature take its course.

Self-thought positive mindset is what can enable any person to strive through any difficult part of one's life. Do whatever it takes that can help you to release the negative emotions when tough times happened to you. Crying is also a very useful tactic for me because, usually, shedding some tears actually acts as a release mechanism for me. Even until my current stage of life, I am not ashamed to share that I can still be a crybaby at times. There is nothing wrong with using whatever techniques or ways there are that make you feel better during the difficult time as long it releases your pressure and makes your mind clearer afterward.

It was also during this difficult stage of my life that I came across the beauty of meditation. Meditation is an in-depth wisdom skill by itself that can be practiced wherever you are, and it is totally free of charge. The simplest form of meditation is just to sit alone in a quiet place and void yourself of all stray thoughts just by observing your own breathing. Even doing so on a daily basis for five to ten minutes can already do wonders to your life in the long run. Whenever you meet with obstacles or failures in your life, try practicing meditation. This will do you great wonders.

In summary, what I can share about failure is that only through failing can you appreciate life better and be grateful for what you already possess. Failure also prepares you for bigger responsibility in the future and makes you a stronger person. The only people who had never failed are people who had never tried before. All people who tried will fail at some point, but the key difference in becoming successful is the attitude you apply after you had failed and whether such failure can enlighten you to become a smarter and wiser person by not repeating the same mistakes again.

Myth that leads to success: if you are scared to fail, you will not fail.

In fact, the exact opposite is what makes it right. When you can face failure with an open heart, ironically, you will fail less. When we have fear in our heart, we will get intangible stress, pressure, and tension; we will not be able to bring out our best performance and potential. Only by facing our life challenges with no fear of failure could we conquer our inner self as well as handle all external uncontrollable circumstances with ease and peace.

COVID-19: As I am writing this book, the world seems strange to everyone, with the lockdowns and curfews causing a lot of tension and uncertainties for humankind. Fear is everywhere, with commoners rushing to supermarkets and shopping online in a fanatic fashion, with the zeal of stocking up the daily necessities as if the Third World War is approaching at our doorstep. This clearly shows the vulnerability of mankind and the intensity of what fear can do. The flight and fight modes are the two mechanisms of human nature when fear strikes. Which one will you choose in critical situations like this? Remember once again, your decision will determine the fate of your future and make an impact to all people that revolve around you. Make the right decision to stay strong, stay brave, and stay positive.

CHAPTER 2

The Beauty of Human Relationship

I DO NOT have any specific talents or skills as a person. Just like the mass population, I was brought up in a normal family, got my tertiary education, and entered society with thousands of graduates looking for a career that will hopefully lead us to our dream life and bright future. The only difference in my choice of path is that instead of looking for a secure, stable job, I decided to focus all my effort in honing my interpersonal skills and envisioning to become a top salesperson in my chosen profession and walking down the challenging path of entrepreneurship. As I built my career and multimillion-dollar portfolio just with the art and skill of selling, I am extremely passionate and excited to share this part of my life journey, hopefully, to inspire the younger generation and those who will like to join in the challenge.

What will come to a surprise to many is that a successful salesperson can easily earn much more than someone in the management role working for a big organization. To be top in sales is not just to have the gift of gab, it involves much more complex skills such as understanding human behavior and psychology. The most difficult stage of sales is to break the ice in the beginning and eventually to build a strong bond and trust throughout the long-lasting cooperation with your customers. Nothing in life can be built without trust, and trust takes years to build but seconds to break. Trust can be so vulnerable, which is why we must never take customers who had supported us along the way for granted. We must constantly remind ourselves to express our gratitude and appreciation to them with absolute sincerity and genuineness. Being able to handle people from all levels with diplomacy will always give you the advantage or edge to thrive in this chosen profession, as nothing monetary can be exchanged until another person is supportive of what you are promoting.

One important attribute that separates the top salespersons from the mediocre mass is their willingness to go through the extra mile. You will always be rewarded in accordance to the value that you are able to bring to others. This is an indisputable fact that all salespersons will have to agree and accept. Just imagine if you are given a sum of money to spend on supporting a chosen salesperson and this reward will naturally be given to the one who you felt can provide you with the highest level of excellent service and someone with a pleasant personality that leave you with good experience and unforgettable memory. Sales is not just a job; it is also a piece of art that can only be mastered by the few who paint their own creation with passion and daily effort.

No one typical sales personality can handle all customers, and there is no fixed formulation to become successful for this career. You need to constantly remain creative and apply flexibility according to the environment and situation. To close a successful deal is hard work and involves many steps, and many salespeople will blame bad luck when they fail to do so. Luck will come to those who work and prepare for it. Luck means meeting the right people at the right situation to promote the right product that he or she is looking for. The more hardworking, prepared, determined, and street-smart you are, the higher your chance of striking the lucky star.

When I set up my second business venture on my own at age twenty-seven, I counted myself very lucky throughout my eighteen years on the entrepreneur path, whereby I was connected with many incredible people who lent me a helping hand along the way. When I first started this business with a very small capital during year 2002, I was lucky to meet Mr. Tan from Eng Soon (please check the success story of Eng Soon), who rented me part of his Tuas factory to store my goods for very low rental per month. This gave me a good strong foothold to keep my expenses low. As a one-woman show, I was doing invoicing, sales, accounting, order processing, and delivery all by myself to keep the ball rolling. Life was very challenging because I just got my second newborn daughter and my eldest daughter also just turned one year old. I will never forget the experience of bringing both of them to my office and breastfeeding my younger baby while simultaneously having to cope with the daily operation of this new start-up. I worked almost sixteen to eighteen hours nonstop every day, sometimes sleeping in the office. This kind of lifestyle lasted for almost two years before I started to employ people to help me. I am this kind of very conservative entrepreneur who is very cautious about cash flow, and I prioritize to pay all suppliers on time to build a good reputation by maintaining other expenses to an absolute minimum. This strategy actually does pay off in the later part of my business venture, as integrity and business ethics are the two main factors that will bring your company to the next horizon. Thinking back, without the trust and support from suppliers and customers who believed in me and were willing to give me a chance, I would not be able to achieve what I have today. No person can be successful on their own. Success needs to be accompanied by many extrinsic and intrinsic factors, of which being able to handle relationships, especially in time of adversity, plays a vital part in determining your level of success.

I have never seen any successful person in this world who makes it without the skill of handling human relationships and getting support for a good cause in what they are trying to build or promote. For any business to be successful, we need to have other people who believe in us and are willing to extend their supporting hand from a monetary aspect. There is no point to invent the best innovative products on this planet if no one wants to buy or own it. Whatever goal you want to achieve in your life, you will need for others to believe in you. And this usually can happen only when you are able to influence the mindset of those people you are connected to in a positive and meaningful fashion, with the objective of striking win-win for all parties.

The ability to negotiate is another vital part of the sales role that can make or break you. There are three main elements revolving all negotiation process, namely time, information, and power. The outcome of whether the negotiation will come out positive or negative is greatly dependent on how good you are to make use of these three elements to your advantage. By having absolute control of the situation with well-prepared information and appropriate timing to your advantage, your battle will already be won by half before any further action needs to be taken. Negotiation usually involves highlighting the pros of your proposal and diminishing or eliminating the cons of what is being suggested. A good negotiator will, in fact, never let the other party feel any discomfort or threat during the negotiation process. Contradictory to this, the receiving party will feel at ease with your suggested proposal and appreciate your effort and good intention to find common ground and solutions to a challenging situation on hand. A master negotiator will leave no room for the other party to put on their defense mechanisms or to dispute what he is negotiating for a good cause. To be a good negotiator means to be fully well prepared and to visualize all possible outcomes during the negotiation process so that one can counteract any sudden outcome with immediate solutions to counter-offer smartly on the negotiation table. This will leave no stone unturned, and throughout my entrepreneurship journey, I had experienced umpteen negotiation deals that ended with powerful triumphant handshaking. The power of being persuasive and convincing during the negotiation process comes along with experience and practice. Exuding confidence, with the right incorporation of laughter to release any built-up tension along the process, usually does the trick most of the time. Practice makes perfect, so the more negotiation deals you handle in your entrepreneur path, the better you will become at it. Do bear in mind that one's negotiation skill is by itself a powerful tool to always get what you want to achieve, but the core principle of the outcome is that whatever is being proposed must strike win-win situation for all parties. Only by sticking to this die-hard principle can each outcome be fruitful, and your relationship with the other party can be long-lasting, concrete, harmonious, and blissful.

Being authentic and charismatic makes you stand out as a person, especially in the sales profession. Usually, the ones who make it to the top in sales for any particular profession are not the smartest or the most talented but the unique species who are authentic and likeable. To understand the true meaning of the word *authentic*, just think of music. Music is something that most people find enticing, but it is not intelligible in the way that many art forms are. The beauty of music is not so much understood intellectually as it is felt in the body. Music engages the instinct, drive, and senses. You can sense its beauty way before you can articulate it. Instincts, drive, and passion are types of knowledge that are built into our body, and every person actually possesses this kind of power in our own unique way. This unique drive within each person is like a burning passion that, when applied in the right direction and harnessed properly, allows our inner potential to reach its peak. Our intellect and our instinct, when working in harmony together, will carry the wisdom of who and what we are supposed to be. Our mind can help this destiny express itself in a controlled and productive way. When your instinct and intellect are in harmony, you lead an authentic life and become who you are meant to be. On the other hand, if we suppress our inner fire of passion, instinct, and drive, we deny life and create a discord between our body and mind. Our body becomes a place of war and turns on itself; our mind becomes tired, and we become slaves of our own body. Sad to mention, most of us are led to a mediocrity mindset and lifestyle by giving up on our authentic self, having to follow the herd instinct so as to be in compliance and be accepted by our peers and society. Being authentic is to embrace the fact that there is intelligence, instinct, and passion contained in our natural drive, which can be harnessed by our intellectual mind. This act of self-creation allows us to reach our highest potential and give us what we uniquely need to give to the world and to achieve anything we want in the world. If we suppress our inner fire, we suppress the energy needed to overcome the obstacles that we may face on the way to reach our highest potential, thereby leading to mediocrity. Being authentic will always position yourself and your business in an irreplaceable position in the competitive world of business. It is just like how many great entrepreneurs in this world built a legacy—when people think of a particular brand, they will naturally link this brand to the authentic founder (for example, Steve jobs to Apple and Bill Gates to Microsoft).

Myth that leads to success: The more you talk about trying to impress and sell yourself, the higher chance of getting the deal.

In fact, the secret to closing a deal is more about empathic listening rather than speaking. As the saying goes, "An empty vessel makes the most noise." Most of the time, the real connection between people happens when you are able to practice empathic listening skills and to provide sound and wise advice or comments based on your best knowledge after analysis and deduction. Always practice the 80/20 rule when you handle your sales profession. For this case, 80 percent of empathy is listening and 20 percent is acute wise talking. No customer likes exchanging any monetary value for something that they will later regret due to their own stupidity to trust or rely on a salesperson who provides inaccurate information or groundless facts with no substance.

COVID-19: Social distancing, working from home, and not to talk to strangers when out shopping for necessities during this COVID-combating period are indirectly making our current world a colder and more isolated and remote place to live in. Aren't we humans supposed to be interactive, communicative herd animals rather than solitary? Why has the COVID situation swapped the current situation, whereby we humans cannot even do the basic fundamentals of life, such as having fun with our peers by having social gatherings, hugging our neighbors, and saying hello to strangers? Doing our daily marketing with our masks on and keeping a one-meter distance to safeguard our life disconnects us from human-to-human interaction and closeness. The irony of life is that we humans tend to be too clever for our own good. We create the best technology possible, thinking that this will make our earth a better place to live in. Are we really doing good for mankind with constant urbanization and modernization without striking a balance from the perspective of humanity? Even family members nowadays prefer to use mobile phones to send messages as the mode of communication rather than talking face-to-face despite living under the same roof. In my opinion, nothing can beat the personal touch. Do remember that we are humans and not robots that can function purely by following strict procedures and protocols. We need compassion, empathy, and a sense of love and trust while we are living in this universe shared by seven billion others of our own species. Human relationships will always surpass all advanced technology— this will be my concluding statement.

CHAPTER 3

The Beauty of Stoicism in Practice

TO THE MISPERCEPTION of many, Stoicism is not a religion. It is just a philosophy of life that can be practiced on daily basis to make us become a better and more conscious person. Stoicism is profound, practical, and useful in our modern life; and throughout my entrepreneur path, I am able to brave through many obstacles and hardships by sticking to the teachings of Stoicism. By mastering Stoicism, you will be able to follow a lifelong principles and protocol that will always guide you through the tough times.

To simplify the concept of Stoicism, let us imagine an egg with its yolk, white, and shell.

> yolk: physics core of Stoicism
> white: ethics
> shell: logic solidity

These three factors are interdependent and need to co-exist in order for the system to function and work well.

Shell (logic): Logic is an art, the rational thinking of cause and effect. A wise man is always a dialectician, for everything is seen through consideration of it in arguments—both what belongs to the topic of physics and what belongs to ethics. Logic is not only the hard shell that hold ethnics and physics together but also the firm and solid art of reasoning that must be mastered in order to engage the two aspects of stoic philosophy.

White (ethics): What acts are appropriate and what acts are non-appropriate? Once we master the art of logic, we can determine our ethics. This, in turn, determines our virtues (which lead to happiness) and vices (which contribute to misery). There are four categories of virtue, namely moderation, justice, courage, and wisdom. On the other hand, the four categories of vice are injustice, cowardice, intemperance, and foolishness. Wisdom is the ability to navigate complex situations in a logical, informed, and calm manner. Temperance is the exercise of self-restraint and moderation in all aspects of life. Justice means treating others with fairness even if they have done wrong. Courage means facing daily challenges with clarity and integrity. Between vice and virtue lies a huge gray area of things that are not necessarily bad or necessarily good that we call by the term *indifferent*. In stoic preaching, indifferent isn't necessarily harmful or contributing to happiness, and how you use these things greatly depend on the actual context, and your ability to reason helps you to decide on your ability to act accordingly to the actual situation faced. From a Stoic standpoint, the goal of life is to smoothly flow along with the natural course.

All things are parts of the one simple system called nature, and any individual life will only be good when it is in harmony with nature. Virtue is in perfect agreement with nature, whereas vice goes against nature. Preferred indifferent includes strength, wealth, pleasure, and good reputation; but these positive attributes do not necessary lead to happiness. On the other hand, nonpreferred indifferent includes disease, weakness, ugliness, poverty, and low reputation; but these negative attributes do not necessary lead to misery either.

Yolk (physics): Stoic physics simply means the understanding of nature. The simple formula of stoic physics is a system of ideas and concepts (matter + pneuma = existence). Matter is anything that our senses can perceive but is described as passive, lifeless, and destroyable. In contrast, pneuma makes the universe alive and cannot be destroyed (e.g., waves of the seas, movements of stars and planets, etc.). Stoics believe that everything around us operates accordingly to a web of cause and effect resulting in a rational structure of the universe that is called the *logos*.

Stoicism can be learned by modern people from all status; historic records during ancient Greek times show it was widely practiced by many, from the poor to the emperor, including luminaries such as Seneca (writer of *The Shortness of Life*), Plato (writer of *The Apology*), Epictetus (writer of *The Enchiridion*), Marcus Aurelius (write of the famous *Meditations*), the great roman emperor who ruled his empire while strictly adhering to stoic teachings, leading to peace and prosperity during his reign.

Minimalism is actually one typical practices of Stoicism that is pursued now by many people from our modern society who realized that having an abundance of material possessions and pursuits might not be the right course to ultimate happiness and fulfillment in life. For myself, I have been practicing to be a minimalist for many years, and I always try to keep material possessions to an absolute minimum. The pursuit of spiritual and intellectual wisdom seems more enticing than the mere possession of material gains. Those who buy luxury goods such as expensive cars or branded goods will soon realize that such purchases can only entice their excitement and pump their adrenaline for a short moment and the excitement and adrenaline rush are never sustainable for long-term happiness. As what I had always shared with many, we cannot bring our wealth or material possessions to our grave. Just imagine our spirit being given a chance to see and feel who comes to our wake when we pass on—our concern by then will be how those people whom we were connected to during our mortal life really viewed us as a person and whether we had lived a meaningful and fruitful life that brought good to humankind. I had seen many classic examples of the wealthy families whereby once the estate holder had passed away without proper allocation of his asset portfolio, fights and quarrels would emerge among the direct relatives. If life is all about seeking material pleasure, then we humans should not have woken up daily in the first place, going after something that, when we come to an end, we will not be able to bring along or something that will not provide any tangible meaning for our life. Instead, we should seek to build our own character and not to seek happiness from material possessions—material things can always be lost for whatever reason, but our character is what will follow us and enable us to survive through all ups and downs in life. What does minimalism have to do with entrepreneurship? Well, minimalists reduce or eliminate all clutter in their lives, which enables them to stay fully focused on their goal and objective. The good practice of keeping everything to a minimum also keeps your business structure lean and trim. Complication does not mean success in business. The lesser bottlenecks you encounter in an organization, the more efficient your team can perform and the better the output will be using a fixed set of resources. It is always a challenge for all organizations to balance between compliance and flexibility, and the compromise point must always be reviewed constantly to ensure smooth, ongoing business.

Stoicism preaches to stop seeking the praise and recognition of other people. There will always be toxic people present in our life who will discourage or even put down dreams that we believe in. There are seven billion people in this universe, and it is not possible for any person to please all of them. Live your own life, and pursue what you think is right. Leave the naysayers alone, for to be honest, no one has the right to comment on something that they themselves do not even have the courage to work on. Even if they had tried this idea and failed, that does not mean that you will not succeed. Maybe it is simply that their way of handling is wrong or the timing is just not right. Before I started writing this book, I did not have Facebook, Instagram, or any social media; I preferred to lead a simple, focused, and fulfilled life based on what I believe in. It is more practical to focus on getting daily concrete results than to get likes and dislikes by many commenters, with thumbs up or down on such platforms that can distract you and sway you away from achieving your goal and objective. Just remember that our happiness and success depend on no one but ourselves. It is always better to be hated for what you are than to be loved for what you are not. To seek approval from others by being someone that is not you will get you nowhere and will never lead to true happiness or success in life. People will never see your struggles along the way. They will only see your success when you reach your peak, and only then will they comment all the nice things in front of you, so why worry so much and be so concerned in the first place?

One big piece of wisdom from the practice of Stoicism is to focus on what you have control over in life. This is so valuable and important that everyone should exercise it if they want to brave through the challenging path of entrepreneurship or any hardships they are facing. We are just humble individuals being trying to survive in this competitive world, and many things that happen in our lives are simply out of our control. We cannot control the behaviors and decisions of our customers or ensure that we will always get their continuous support in business. As we all know, nothing is permanent in life, and outcomes do change invariably according to many uncontrollable factors. What we can control, however, is our thoughts and actions on how to provide the best possible service to our valuable customers so that such frequency can inherently influence their mindset to support us in return.

Once again, I will like to emphasize that the law of attraction does exist, and you will eventually get what you deserve if you visualize hard enough to get what you want and put these affirmations and visualizations into concrete daily actions.

Anger is one of the seven deadly sins (greed, pride, lust, anger, gluttony, sloth, and envy). These are also known as the capital vices, and they are greatly emphasized, analyzed, and debated in Stoicism. If anyone wants to understand more about the Christian theology of seven sins in a simplified and illustrative manner, I highly recommend the film *Seven* starring Brad Pitt and Morgan Freeman, directed by David Fincher during the year 1995. This is one of the best movies I have watched that highlights the seven sins in a thrilling and entertaining fashion. Anger is a destructive energy by itself that should be destroyed immediately and should not even be allowed to reach the level of controlling. From the point of Stoicism, anger can drive you to the state of insanity, causing you to conduct unnatural acts that are unreasonable and damaging to society and the people around you. When we allow anger to overcome us, we become its slave as it blinds our vision to see the truth toward the future. The consequences of our actions for the moment effectively override the rationale of our higher selves and the wisdom of reasoning what is right and wrong. Understand that anger is a binary emotion that is impelling and cannot be slowed down. Anger is also contagious in a negative fashion and motivates revenge and retaliation. Throughout my entrepreneurship, I had made some wrong decisions as a result of anger, and they are all painful lessons that created a certain degree of damage that should not be overlooked. Practice mindfulness, meditation, listening to music, and even reading art such as poetry and literature to curb anger before it escalates to a deadly level. Always delay the urge to take any immediate actions at the spur of anger to avoid making decisions that will make you regretful later. Be mindful of what we speak when we are in a fit of anger because words, once spoken, cannot be taken back. Entrepreneurship involves the cultivation of high emotional intelligence, and practicing compassion and forgiveness are the most effective ways to counteract any angry situation during the tough times of your journey. Anger is itself a very strong emotion, but the best time to reflect on our own rage is when we are not angry. By allowing ourselves the consciousness and awareness of what anger can do to our life and the critical decisions we make, we can all prime our minds and feelings to be able to choose a gentler path when we get angry. Anger can sometimes be put to good use from a business perspective, as this is often a signal that things are not moving to the right direction. By all means, feel angry when you feel threatened and intimated in business by a fierce competitor. But instead of lashing out, leverage the energy and power of anger to make something creative and productive for your business. Take this emotional state and convert it into a fiery positive drive that channels this powerful signal to the universe to receive positive outcomes in return.

Most of the time, the negative emotions we experience are just the results of our negative thoughts on how we interpret things. There are so many situations in my entrepreneur life when I turned the tables around by practicing positive thoughts in negative situations. It is only through our own powerful positive thoughts that we can subconsciously influence people around us to change the outcome of a business decision from unfavorable to favorable. This can be done through many years of devotion to the practice of Stoicism.

The practice of Stoicism teaches all entrepreneurs to prepare for any negative outcome by constantly practicing negative visualization to anticipate the not-so-good with the intention to act with resilience when tough time arrives. Doing business is just like fighting a war and is more like wrestling than slow dancing in comparison of sports. True entrepreneurs are always well prepared against the accidental and the unforeseen, and are not apt to fall. The secret to success in business lies largely in our ability to stay resilient in the face of adversity and setbacks. Successful entrepreneurs will always see adversity as opportunity rather than as problems, and they will practice absolute flexibility to make appropriate adjustments in order to win the ultimate battle.

Stoicism involves seeking personal improvement, understanding the importance of the shortness of life, and practicing humility. Time is the essence in business, and only by realizing how little time we have will all entrepreneurs treasure the twenty-four hours given daily to maximize this time frame and push ourselves to the limit. Seeking continuous improvement is the only way to make you always stay in the lead within your competitive industry. To stay humble, kind, and compassionate regardless of where you are in the path of entrepreneurship and social circle will never go wrong. Practice constant gratification as preached by Stoicism, for whatever we have in our life that is bestowed by the Higher One and people who support us along the way. Never let our pride and overpowering ego get the better of us in the business world, as this will inadvertently lead to self-destruction.

Myth that leads to success: Ego is a person's sense of self-esteemed and net worth.

The hard truth is that most people learn from their failures (a state of humility), and people seldom learn when they are successful (a high-ego state). Only by removing ego completely can we strip ourselves to be completely naked in front of our own mirrors and be left with what is real. Ego often blinds us to seek the truth, and it makes us assume that our limited knowledge and know-how is above all and always right. Most of the time, there is no absolute right or wrong in how we handle things in life; there is just how different people handle the same situations differently according to their experience and wisdom. All greatness come from humble beginnings, and the most successful people are usually the ones who are always in low profile, leading the simplest yet most meaningful lifestyles possible.

COVID-19: We cannot control what is happening to the outside world, but we can definitely control our own thoughts and actions about the current COVID situation. Apply a daily positive, cheerful attitude and mindset while we are all locked down at home. Current COVID situation acts as an awakening call for all people, and it has let us understand the beauty of nonmaterialistic matters such as freedom, social connection, and even staying safe and healthy for one extra day. One of the Stoic exercises is to do voluntary acts of discomfort such as sleeping on the floor, disconnecting yourself completely from social media for a period of time, taking cold showers to boost your endurance power. These acts remind you to be grateful and to appreciate what you already possess. Let us all take this lockdown period from the Stoic angle and push our limit to challenge this trying time as one united universe.

CHAPTER 4

The Beauty of Forming Good Habits

AS THE SAYING goes, "Humans are creatures of habit." So how long does it take for a good habit to be formed? The median time to build a solid recurring habit is to take consistent action for sixty-six consecutive days without fail until it forms part of your routine life. Doing something consistently for sixty-six days acts as a psychological motivator and subconsciously propels the person to automatically achieve the final reward. This technique works wonders simply due to the release of dopamine (the feel-good hormone) when we accomplish something successfully in our life. The loss-aversion effect—which means as the days go by, the state associated with us not doing the habit right will cause us to feel that we have more to lose if we do not follow through (for example, the desire of losing one hundred dollars is greater than our desire to gain one hundred dollars)—also aids us to benefit after the sixty-six-day time frame so that we persist in sticking with the habit. Our thoughts are just infinite possibilities of who we can be. The thought we act on will reflect our true nature. When our thoughts are in line with our actions, we live in peace. But once we are unaligned, we live in chaos. To have a more aligned life, we need to take control of our daily habits. It is difficult to break a bad habit unless you can cultivate a good habit to replace it. Good habits are always hard to form but easy to live with, and bad habits are easy to get addicted to but hard to get rid of.

So what are some of the good habits of successful entrepreneurs?

Waking up early: I have been staying disciplined to wake up early between 5:00–6:00 a.m. for many years. When I first decided to form this habit as part of my daily lifestyle, it was quite challenging for me, as I might stay up late due to work-related matters, sometimes way past midnight. My kind of business also required me to do constant travelling, and time differences and jet lag due to these time zone differences really posed great challenges to achieve this. The minimum eight hours' sleep per night theory had been much debated in recent years. It is debated by many recent scientific studies that it is more the quality rather than the quantity of sleep you get per day that really matters. In fact, how much sleep one needs depends on factors such as age, chronotypes, physical activity, seasonality, genetics, sleep drive and circadian entrainment, and many other factors. I must admit, due to my hectic agenda, I am sleep-deprived most of my life if compared to a person with a normal sleep cycle. I had to juggle between working and schooling as a teenager and then followed that by choosing the entrepreneur path whereby I got to work nonstop, even on public holidays, for long hours. Maybe because I am used to such sleeping pattern, I can do pretty well with a minimum of five to six hours of sleep every night. What impresses many is my ability to stay fully energized and motivated throughout my many years of consistently short sleep. The tricks to staying fully energized are to have daily goals that keep your spirit up and going and to do lots of exercise with proper nutrition. It is very important for me to keep my room completely dark, quiet, and cool during my short sleeping duration. Some of the other factors that affect sleep quality are sleep latency, how much deep and REM sleep you get, electromagnetic fields, your psychological state, wake-up frequency, what time you sleep and wake up, well-being in the morning when you wake up, level of performance during your active moment, basal heart rate, and heart rate variability (HRV). Timing when you go to bed actually has a huge impact on the overall quality of your sleep and how much sleep you need. Some hours of sleep are more productive than others, and you can gain a higher quality from them. Every living organism, including human beings, has some sort of sleep-wake cycle and circadian rhythm. It is linked with the day-night cycle of the planet, and it affects all of your physiological processes including sleep. After darkness, our body will start to produce melatonin, which is the sleep hormone that prepares our body to feel tired and to go into a rest mode. This then prepares our body for recovery by boosting growth hormone production and autophagy. Humans who have a high level of growth hormone usually age slower and stay healthier throughout their life span. This is the reason why we should avoid exposure to blue light from our handphones and computers before bed, as this greatly disrupts the production of melatonin and disrupts our circadian rhythm, leading to poor quality sleep. Poor quality sleep, in the long run, can lead to depression, diabetes, cancer, hypertension, neurodegeneration, and obesity. For people who want to control their weight, sleep deprivation actually increases the hunger hormone ghrelin, which increases fat deposition, especially around our stomach area. Melatonin production usually starts at 10:00–11:00 p.m. and peaks at 2:00 a.m. This happens in conjunction with the activity of other repair hormones (such as growth hormone), and autophagy also increases around that time. Cortisol (the awakening hormone) levels start rising around 5:00–7:00 a.m. and peak at 9:00 a.m., whereas melatonin drops at dawn completely to make space for cortisol to wake our body up. Exposure to sunlight during daytime is important for our body to produce melatonin at night because the UV light from our sun helps to lower cortisol and promotes the conversion of serotonin to melatonin as night falls. Coffee is best consumed between the time you wake up till 12:00 p.m., as caffeine can stay in your body as long as to five to six hours. This can affect your sleep if you consume coffee later in the day. In summary, I highly recommend avoiding sleep deprivation, as this will lead to forgetfulness, lack of focus, reduced productivity, and other health-related issues, such as insulin resistance, prediabetes, Alzheimer's disease, metabolic syndrome, obesity, and even higher mortality rate. I cannot stress how important it is for all entrepreneurs to ensure that they understand the fundamentals of how the sleep cycle works in order to maximize our precious daily twenty-four hours to have optimum productivity.

Physical activity: Exercise is the most valuable natural miracle drug for our body. Exercise is a keystone habit that provides a lot of benefits, such as maintaining our healthy body weight, building more muscle, and helping fight against a lot of terminal diseases such as high blood pressure, heart problems, and diabetes. People who exercise regularly seem to stay happier and more motivated in the long run, and regular physical activities do help to fight against mental issues such as depression, insomnia, memory loss, and Alzheimer's and Parkinson's diseases. This is because our body naturally produces hormones such as serotonin, endorphins, and brain-derived neurotrophic factor (BDNF) when we are physically active. In turn, this helps reduce our stress levels, improves our mood, aids in better sleep, improves our cognitive capability, and stimulates HGH (human growth hormone) production, which retard aging. Muscle makes up one-third of our body weight, and how we treat our muscles on a daily basis will determine how they will grow or at least retard the shrinking of muscle mass as we age. Muscle cells burn more calories than fat cells, which is why we must do the right combination of different forms of exercise in order to have optimum results. Weight and strength training help build our muscle mass and preserve our bone density. On the other hand, cardio exercise improves our lung and heart function and is effective to keep our weight in check. It can also burn some serious belly fat if carried out on a disciplined regular basis of four to five times per week. High-intensity interval training also proves to be very effective for busy entrepreneurs who cannot find time to do long-haul cardio exercises such as jogging and swimming, as it takes only about fifteen to thirty minutes for a full effective workout conducted three times a week.

Nutrition: Being in the food industry most of my life, I am a passionate foodie. Exploring nice and delicious delicacies whenever I travel extensively has naturally formed part of my lifestyle and hobby. Cooking and creating innovative recipes also form a part of my addictive passion and favorite pastime. Dining with family, close associates, and friends forms a big part of my social circle's lifestyle, and many people who know me as a person always wonder how I keep my current physique despite my age, the number of children I had, my hectic business lifestyle, plus consuming all the good rich food, which makes it real challenging to enjoy the best of both worlds. My secret? It all lies in the way you indulge and having a balanced diet afterward. For example, if I know that I am going to have a big dinner event tomorrow night, I will skip breakfast and have a moderate lunch followed by that sumptuous dinner. I will always try to eat within the sixteen- and eight-hour window wherein I will fast for sixteen hours the day before and eat within the eight hours window period the next day after my first meal. Most of the time, I will skip breakfast before my gym regimen early in the morning and then break my fast around noontime and to take my dinner around 6:00–7:00 p.m. In this way, my insulin level will not spike up frequently by constant digestion of food and this also makes me more energetic throughout the day, since food digestion does bring certain stress mechanisms to our body and leads to fatigue and tiredness during this time frame.

Intermittent fasting does affect your circadian rhythm as well, as it is a dieting method by controlling the time you eat during the day. A feeding-fasting rhythm enhances the robustness or amplitude of the oscillation of circadian activator and repressor components. Therefore, if fasting is done in the proper manner, it should improve your quality of sleep as well. In fact, the length of the fasting period should parallel the length of sleep. Low insulin is one of the effects of intermittent fasting, which leads to better secretion of melatonin that leads to better sleep. There are many benefits of intermittent fasting, such as reducing insulin (the fat-deposit hormone that promotes diabetes), increasing your growth hormone (which makes you look better and live longer) and promoting the production of brain-derived neuro factor (a key hormone for growing new brain cells). It also helps you lose weight and gain muscle, and it enhances your cognitive performance.

In my opinion, compared to many kinds of dieting plans such as Atkins, paleo, vegan, Dukan, Zone, low carb, low fat, and even the recent popular ketogenic diet (for most of which I had done quite a bit of research and in-depth study), I still find intermittent fasting the most effective and easy-to-adapt approach. All you need to do is to exert some discipline to refrain from eating out of the window period; once you cultivate this simple habit into your daily lifestyle, your hunger hormone ghrelin will gradually go away, and you will no longer feel hungry most of the time. The good thing about this fasting diet is that you can enjoy whatever nice cuisine you want during the feeding period as long you are eating in moderation. For most of the other diet methods mentioned above, you will need to watch out what you are putting into your mouth and constantly count your calorie intake, which many busy individuals find difficult to sustain in the long run.

I would like to highlight the importance of consuming prebiotics, probiotics, and fiber for our gut health. Probiotics are all kinds of fermented food such as natto, sauerkraut, tempeh, yogurt, and kimchi. Prebiotics are mostly plant-based foods that are high in fiber (such as garlic, onion, asparagus, oats, leek, apples, seaweed, avocado, and tomatoes) that cannot be easily digested by our intestines and can aid in the absorption of probiotics. There are so many health benefits for eating probiotic and prebiotic foods, with prevention of leaky guts and inflammation being at the top of the list. Inflammation is closely associated with a lot of health issues such as stroke, heart problems, type 2 diabetes, and cancer. It is important to maintain healthy daily pooping, and this can be easily achieved by drinking two big glasses of lemon water first thing in the morning when you wake up or drinking apple cider vinegar once in the morning and once before bedtime. Both chia seeds and psyllium husk are excellent source of fiber. They can be easily incorporated into our daily diet by adding them into our beverages (such as coffee, tea, and plain water). Chia seeds can be sprinkled onto our salads and yogurt, whereas psyllium husk can be used widely for baking and cooking, especially in keto diets, to boost our fiber intake. Sugar is the silent killer of our modern diet today, and sugar can be found hidden in more than 90 percent of the processed food that you can find on the shelves of our supermarkets today. A lot of sugar is actually ingested into our body through fluids rather than from solid foods, so do be mindful of the beverages you consume daily. Indulge in processed food to the absolute minimum, and try to add more whole foods with single ingredients that can be eaten raw.

What can be more important to an entrepreneur than to fuel our body with the right nutrients so that we can have optimum power to complete our challenging daily tasks on hand? Health is wealth, and every person only has one body, so if we are able to stay disciplined and cultivate our good daily habits of sleep, diet, and exercise, longevity and sustainability are not unreachable goals despite whatever busy schedule any individual possess.

Reading: Reading is the fuel that feeds our mind, and just like our muscles, our brain will stop developing and improving the day we stop all intellectual nourishment. I will touch on this topic in a deeper level in the later chapter on seeking continuous improvement.

Goal-setting: Daily and long-term goal-setting are a must for all entrepreneurs who want to succeed in their pursuit. I can still remember when I started my entrepreneur path during the year 2002. My one-sentence vision was "Build a one-stop supply chain specializing in processed meat segment and become the market leader of this chosen industry." This sentence became my obsessive daily spiritual scripture, and I practiced the law of attraction and affirmation technique consistently without fail, with the absolute belief that this mission will be achieved. Most successful individuals write daily journals as their keystone habit. We do become what we think and write about most of the time. Always be result-oriented rather than time-oriented, and focus on top-priority activities that will give you the optimum results. Make use of the 80/20 rule once again, and remain focused and disciplined till you achieve your most important goals before tackling the other less-important ones. Setting goals is not difficult, but it is the consistent daily action of doing the same thing over and over again that poses the big challenge. Some of the techniques that can be used to help in sustainability include the following: alerting someone who is in full support of your idea and getting them to motivate or push you whenever you start to slacken, building up a buddy system with someone who wants to achieve the same objective as you are, writing out this goal in big print and pasting them in prominent areas of your workplace and home so that this can act as constant reminders, and practicing the law of attraction by imagining that you already achieved it and imagining all the benefits and rewards that you get out of it.

Self-discipline is the basic foundation habit that makes everything possible. Self-discipline is simply the ability to make yourself do what you should do when you should do it, whether you feel like it or not. I have never seen anyone succeed without mastering this trait of self-discipline. Only through acquiring this skill of self-discipline can you gain mastery in whatever you want to achieve. On average, it takes a person about ten thousand hours of focused effort to attain mastery on whatever skill or knowledge one wants to acquire. It is only through putting in consistent effort to focus on one thing and repeating the process over and over but expecting different results that this is made possible. Without self-discipline, no person will be able to achieve this level of mastery.

Myth that leads to success: Conformity to the standard norm and following what works for others will not go wrong, and you will be on the safe side.

I am one such person who always likes to think out of the box and to challenge the status quo. I do not believe in hearsay on what will work out, and I will only adhere to habits that I believe in after detailed research and going through my thought process. I would like to share this real story of mine about the taboo whereby all women need to take maternity leave for two to three months after birth and to observe certain practices such as not showering or washing your hair for a certain time frame, not moving around or being physically active, avoiding certain foods, eating specific tonic confinement food that can be quite high in carbs and fats, etc. It is believed that if we do not observe such practices, we will suffer certain health complications such as rheumatism, arthritis, and chronic pain whenever the weather turns cold or when we reach our older age. All my four kids are natural births without epidural, and I started working the third day after I gave birth without taking any extra maternity leave. I simply could not afford the luxury of having a long maternity leave due to my commitment and deep sense of responsibility toward my business and valuable customers. As of today, my eldest daughter is already nineteen, and my youngest is approaching ten years of age. I still feel as fit as when I was in my twenties without experiencing any side effects due to my rebellious act of going against the traditional convention. My conclusion is that it all boils down to your daily good habits of regular exercising, eating properly, having a positive outlook of life, and living a fulfilled and motivated life—these are the key factors to keep your physique and mind in tip-top condition. We people decide our own destiny and should only carry out habits that we act upon based on our wisdom after fact-finding and not just following blindly purely for the sake of compliance or herd instinct.

COVID-19: This is the best time for any individual to think positively and cultivate good habits—we are all locked down and working from home. What can be more appropriate timing to start journaling, to set our next big goal, and to finish whatever is still hanging in our bucket lists? No exercise and eating unhealthily during lockdown period? Sorry, folks, no excuses please! There are loads of YouTube videos that teach you how to do workouts from home and how to cook simple healthy meals. We all now have the luxury of extra time due to cut-downs on traveling to and from work. Plan a routine, and stick by it till the lockdown period is over. You will be able to transform and see a new version of yourself who will become more radiant and attractive. Only ignorant people will expect to see different results by doing the same habits over and over again. Learn to live wise, and learn to live well. Move out of your comfort zone, and start working your butt off to attain amazing results that will blow your mind once you achieve them.

CHAPTER 5

The Beauty of Saying No

MOST STEREOTYPICAL PEOPLE think that to always say yes means being polite and kind, conferring themselves the beautiful title of Ms. or Mr. Nice. This is definitely a misperception, as time is precious for everyone (*The Shortness of Life* by Seneca beautifully explains this and can truly enlighten anyone who is wasting their time on unfruitful activities) since we cannot buy this commodity nor can we turn back the clock. History will never repeat itself, and if you are not able to have a clear directive on how to prioritize your own life and say yes only to important agendas that will improve or make your life happier, then I am sorry to comment that you will lose out to those who will. Sometimes it can be so difficult to say no, especially to your close friends or loved ones, for fear of hurting their feelings or feeling left out in a social circle. We tend to behave in a "social proof" fashion so that we can be accepted by the norm and not feel left out. However, history has proven to us time and again that people who leave a legacy are usually the ones who choose to walk a path different from the rest. This is especially true when you study about the successful stories of most entrepreneurs and how they, understanding the essence of time, will selectively choose those activities that are beneficial or meaningful before they will act on them. They are usually the minority who will defy all the naysayers and choose a challenging path, such that most people cannot anticipate why they are doing so in the first place. The highest level of courage that anybody can possess is never to use force or power to get what they want in life. The ultimate level of courage is to be able to stand up for what you believe is right and to go against all odds and prove your fact through positive and practical actions. We always like to follow our herd instinct just to be on the safe side for most of the choices we make in our life. What we fail to understand in a deeper level is that life is unpredictable, and choosing the path most people had gone through does not guarantee a stable or extraordinary outcome. On the contrary, choosing a path that is never experienced by others does not mean it will lead to disaster. We just need to use our wisdom and follow our heart while applying real courage to walk a path that we believe can fulfill our destiny. This is often easier said than done, as people are mostly driven and dictated by our fear of uncertainty and of what the unknown future holds for us. Those who dare to say no, especially during time of adversity, will ultimately unleash the unlimited power to choose their own destiny and lead themselves to freedom of life in all aspects. Another hindrance that stops us from saying no is our psychological mechanism of fear of losing out if we were to reject someone's kind offer. When we are approached with an option or offer, our brain is just brought up since our youth to overthink and overanalyze, most of the time causing us to have the natural reaction of having a difficulty to reject the option open to us. If you want to make it as a successful entrepreneur, learning to train your mind to stay firm and guard your precious time for more focused deep work that leads to your ultimate goals are critical decisions that you need to learn. It is also very important that you mingle with the right social circles that can lead you to the right direction rather than wasting your time on people who will only put your dreams down and not able to provide you with any constructive advice or practical support. The worst kind of people to involve yourself with are those toxic persons who will bombard you with all the negative energy and drain away your positive energy. Keep a safe social distance from individuals who constantly put you down, and surround yourself with positive people. Then your life will be in bliss and abundance. Saying no at the appropriate time only makes your firm character and great quality stand out among the crowd and will gain the respect of other people who really want the best for you and admire your courage of knowing what you want in your life.

Learning to say no helps a lot in time management, which is the process of planning and exercising conscious control of time spent on specific activities with three objectives in mind: increased effectiveness, efficiency, and productivity. As time is precious for all, specifically entrepreneurs with tight daily agendas, learn to delegate and outsource the not-so-important but time-consuming tasks, always plan ahead, minimize interruptions, and multitask. Focusing only on deep work without distractions for around two to four hours per day is proven to be more effective than working for a full eight hours with lots of disturbance and lacking in focus.

One of the most difficult decisions in my entrepreneurship was to decide which listed group I wanted to sell my eighteen years of effort to when I was given two offers from one Swiss and one Netherlands listed group simultaneously. They were both sound companies that approached me with absolute transparency and sincerity. Walking away from a good deal in business and learning to reject and say no involves courage and diplomacy. Most of the time, it is not the process of saying no but the way you phrase and express yourself during the process that really matters. No person or organization likes to be rejected when after something that they look forward to, so we must always practice empathy when we extend our rejection to other people, whether from a business or personal perspective. I had also been rejected by others during my entrepreneurship enough times, but I learned to practice a big heart and accept all rejection with grace and understanding. This will always allow you to go far and maintain a sound reputation in your social circle. And who knows? What goes around will come around, and we might just cross paths again with those whom we get rejected by or those whom we had rejected before.

Myth that lead to success: Settle for second best to play safe if you cannot get the best.

Always aim for the very best in your life, especially in critical decisions that determine your future. It is tempting to settle for second best for fear that you will lose everything if you fail to get the best. Learn to resist the temptation of being lured into the comfort zone of life, which will cause you to lose your direction to fight for what you want the most in your life. Say no to the path that gives you convenience, say no to the path that kills your creativity, and say no to the temptation of material pursuit until you have really reached your destination of real entrepreneurship. Most of the successful people will say no 99 percent of the time and get it perfectly right for the 1 percent that they set their eyes on.

COVID-19: Say no to the constant negative news being constantly broadcasted, and say no to all the fake news that are bombarding our mobile phones and social media. Our world likes to broadcast more negative news as headlines in comparison to positive news, as this will naturally attract more viewers. We cannot change the reality of current COVID situation, but we definitely can decide what we want to digest daily into our spiritual mind. We should not be ignorant of what is going on in our earth, but neither should we be so engrossed in the negativities surrounding us, which leads to panicky and irrational acts of nonsensibility. Why worry about a situation that is already fixed and cannot be changed? Why not focus on matters that we can control within the scope of our ability and influence? No point crying over spilled milk, and no point to live in fear of the fact that not all things in this universe have an answer to our woes. Learn to live strong by standing tall during this lockdown period, with absolute faith and belief that this COVID epidemic shall pass and we will be able to lead our normal lives again very soon, with a greater sense of wisdom and conviction to make our world a better place to live.

CHAPTER 6

The Beauty of Thinking Big
but Taking Small Steps

ALL SUCCESSFUL ENTREPRENEURS start with a big idea—with a conviction so deep that it triggers their inner burning desire to take massive daily actions. They will dream about this big idea day and night, ultimately leading them to put in their best daily effort to cultivate aggressive action plans that finally lead to the success of whatever they want to build. There are never unattained big goals; only lazy people who dwell on those goals but never put in effort to make their dreams come true. Procrastination is one of the great weaknesses in most people, which results from pure habitual laziness or carelessness. Remember my earlier sharing of anger from the seven sins—procrastination is a form of sloth or an act of laziness. To overcome procrastination, basically you need to understand first which of the four categories you belong to, namely: (1) anxious, (2) fun, (3) with plenty of time, or (4) perfectionist. Anxious procrastinators are usually people who have poor time management and are overambitious. They overstretch themselves, scheduling more work than they can cope with, leading to stress and anxiety, which eventually leads to procrastination as an act of denial. The solution for this group of procrastinators is to balance their life to slot in fun or downtime for rest and relaxation. Fun procrastinators usually do not have a focused and will-powered mind to work on their specific task. To counteract fun procrastination, the best way is to give in to your desire to procrastinate, but instead of doing the most dreaded task, working on a less dreaded task that is lower priority. By doing this, you can still be productive in some way and still strike a win-win situation for all, with the intention of at least completing a portion of the workload. Procrastinators with plenty of time usually feel that the deadline is always still far away, or they never have the intention to provide a deadline to accomplish the task they set themselves to accomplish. The best solution for this is to share plans with your families or close friends, as such public commitment will subconsciously motivate you to achieve these goals by having others track the progress. The last type of procrastinators are perfectionists, who are always striving for the best and thereby constantly criticizing their own work. The fear of failing or not being able to meet others' standards and expectations can be so overwhelming that perfectionist procrastinators are not able to start or keep anything going. Unlike the other three kinds of procrastinators, being a perfectionist procrastinator can sometimes be perceived as a positive situation, since they fantasize about doing a perfect job; and so long they do not have a tight deadline, they usually can produce amazing results. Perfectionist procrastinators must learn to de-stress and let loose so as not to give themselves a hard time leading to health issues and complication.

Self-belief is an important actualization process that all entrepreneurs need to practice to sustain their big visions. If you yourself cannot believe you can do it, then no one in the world can. Have absolute faith in what you want to achieve big, and take daily steps to make this happen. Always have your end in mind so that you can still move toward your goal in baby steps even when the situation is not favorable. Rome was not built overnight, and all big ideas must always start somewhere. Build your momentum toward achieving this big goal by making concrete plans and executing these step by step. Just imagine yourself planning to climb Mount Kinabalu, the highest mountain in the Malaysian region. You cannot simply reach the summit unless you make the consistent baby steps. This illustration applies perfectly to all entrepreneurs who want to start something on their own. When you want to complete a two-thousand-piece jigsaw puzzle, you will find it intimidating if you look at it in the big spectrum. However, if you just practice chunking and breaking it down into smaller parts and focusing on that specific area, you will feel that it is more achievable and it can be measured and visualized in a more tangible fashion. By focusing on conquering the big mission in structured, disciplined fashion, in no time you will reach the summit of wherever you want to go. You are the average of the five people that you interact with most of the time, so choose your social circle wisely. The truth is, if you surround yourself with successful individuals, your chance of achieving your big vision and big goal will be high in comparison to if you surround yourself with mediocre people or individuals who will just complain, condemn, criticize, and put the blame of their failure on external circumstances or the environment but never reflect on themselves.

I can still remember how during the year 2003, one year after setting up my company, I had this big ambitious goal to represent one of the world's largest collagen casing brands within the Singapore and Malaysia region. I dreamed of this day and night, and I found ways and means to move toward this big goal. Finally, opportunity knocked on my door, and we were given one chance to prove our ability by competing with their current distributor on a nonexclusive arrangement. I ground and hustled for one whole year and managed to grow the sales sevenfold within the one-year time frame, completely crushing their official appointed distributor. Their exclusive distributor had been working with this multinational company for more than two decades before I entered the processed meat industry. Our supplier was completely blown away, and we were then officially appointed as their exclusive distributor for Singapore and Malaysia and still remain so even after acquisition by the listed group. This experience taught me a priceless lesson in life, which is that nothing is impossible in life. Humility will always triumph over egotism. As we were new in the industry and so hungered for business, we would always put ourselves in a very humble position and put the interest of our customers at heart. In contrast, the current distributor that had this exclusivity for many years was ego-driven. I cannot help but keep think about our childhood educational story about the rabbit and tortoise race. You do not need to be the most talented in your field; you just need to believe in one big idea and focus intensely to make it happen. Do not ever mix up the concept of thinking big as having a big ego. A big ego will eventually lead to arrogance and self-destruction in whatever you build. Stay humble, stay grounded, stay focused.

Myth that lead to success: Big thinkers are not realistic and are impractical; they are just NATO (no action, talk only) and braggers.

Those who dare to dream big will have the chance to win big. Those who dare not even dream will be grounded where they are, waiting for the strong tides to wash them to the deep ocean and drowning when crisis arrives. Chances of advancement will be close to zero for people with no big ambition. We are all given equal opportunities and equal numbers of hours every day to build our dreams. If you start your vision big and far, you will end up far. If you start it small and shallow, then it will be where you land. Learn to think like an eagle and not like other small birds. An eagle flies high and alone. They have accurate vision and will not divert their attention from whatever goals they set their eyes on. No one can guarantee your success for your big idea, including your good self; but at the very least, you will die with no regrets if you have done your very best to maintain the attitude of an eagle spirit.

COVID-19: The big dream for everyone from all parts of our world is that the lockdown, quarantine, and isolation period will soon be over; that we can all go back to our normal social lives; and that we can find a vaccine against this coronavirus. This COVID episode should be an awakening call for all people, for us to ponder about what is really important for our earth and what we can do to make our world a better place to live in. One person's power might be limited, but if every nation educates their citizens to take care of our lovely planet and to practice compassion for humankind, I am sure the big vision of making our earth a more wonderful place can be achieved. We might not meet many people in this universe this lifetime, but we are all interconnected, breathing the same air, and now experiencing the same COVID epidemic disaster. If you can innovate or create any big idea that can serve mankind better, you will be a multimillionaire or even a billionaire in no time.

CHAPTER 7

The Beauty of Living in the Present and Practicing Gratification

I CAN BEHAVE like a kid at times and love all Walt Disney cartoons. The wise tortoise master Oogway of *Kung Fu Panda* said this beautiful iconic phrase, "Yesterday is history, tomorrow is mystery, but today is a gift. That is why we call it the present." People live in fear when we think about the future, which poses uncertainty, and we live in unhappiness when we think of the good old days that realistically might not come back anymore. Not many people can really live in the present with absolute contentment and bliss. There are so many classic cases whereby one only realizes how someone is so dear and important in one's life when this person is gone. We humans are strange creatures that do not treasure or appreciate the present but like to regret about our past actions and imagine a better future.

Why is it so difficult to live in the present? We are such complex species in that our daily moods can be affected by our state of mind, which most of the time tends to overthink and overanalyze. Our physique's condition and external factors that we are unable to control also draw away our attention from focusing on our present consciousness. Daily meditation, as I shared in my earlier chapter, is an excellent way to calm our mind and ground us to our present moment. Our human system needs to be constantly kept in check to have balance between yin and yang. Only then can we attain tranquility of the mind. No entrepreneur can successfully execute any solid plan or make any wise decision unless they have a clear, calm mind with not too much clutter. In this modern society that we are living in, we are often so distracted by so many happenings that cause us to lose our focus to spend time with our inner self. The most difficult kind of lifestyle to sustain in our fast-moving technological era is the lifestyle of simplicity and non-complexity. Ironically, when you climb your social ladder to a certain level, you will realize that one does not need so many material things to stay happy and successful. This is the reason so many successful entrepreneurs become philanthropists—to achieve the state of mind that is self-actualization. Self-actualizing individuals are usually very natural, appreciative, creative, and self-reliant people who possess a great sense of humor. They live in the present and perceive reality accurately and fully and are receptive toward themselves and others.

Out of the ten chapters, this chapter is the most abstract and difficult to express in language because living in the present is a purely spiritual state of mind that can only be felt and experienced rather than taught and shared. It is proven that about 50 percent of our time when we stay awake is not in the present mode. Our mind will easily lose focus and concentration to be swayed toward the past or the future. We must constantly remind ourselves to step out of self-talk that leads to negativity. In our modern society, success is often quantified by our social status, our position and influence in our social circle, and the monetary and material things we possess. However, such ownership does not mean that it will lead to ultimate happiness or inner peace. I had come across many people who possess such high social statuses but are in the state of constant unhappiness and even depression.

What is mindfulness, and how do you practice and improve on this? Mindfulness is the ability to know what is happening in your head without getting carried away by it. This simply means that you are in full control of your emotion and reaction toward any given situation rather than being affected by it. Daily meditation practices such as simple breathing techniques, experiencing the serenity and tranquility of nature (such as strolling by the park or beach in the early morning before any social connection or activity), spending quality quiet moments alone just to be in the state of stillness and calmness (yin element). This self-reflection acts to balance our constant state of action and hyperactive mind (yang element) and gives our mind ample space to be in control of our own outward reaction to the universe. Connection with other people through physical touch, empathic listening, and doing daily kind and compassionate acts also improve your practice of living in the present, as self-centeredness and boredom can trigger our restless mind to the mode of excessive negative overthinking, leading to depression, anxiety, and compulsive behaviors such as gambling, alcoholism, drug addiction, overeating, and low work performance.

Say thank you every morning the moment we wake up to express our gratefulness of what we possess and that we are still alive to pursue our own dreams and to help people around us to fulfill theirs. Practicing gratification first thing every morning helps us to kick-start our day with positivity, optimism, and good feeling. When we express gratification for all things that we have and to accept with grace what we do not have, we will be living in the absolute present moment with complete bliss and happiness.

Throughout my entrepreneurship, due to my very hectic lifestyle (especially at the beginning stage), it was really difficult to practice mindfulness and to be at peace with myself, especially during the challenging moments when I was constantly bombarded with daily incoming business matters that needed immediate attention. To attain this state of mind will involve a lot of willpower and discipline to put aside quality time for oneself no matter how busy your daily schedule is. This sacred time allocation for your spiritual mind enhancement applies the same mindset as you cultivate the habit to exercise and eat well. You have to start somewhere and somehow in order to enjoy the lifelong benefit of mindfulness practice. You will be amazed by how long-term and deep mindfulness practice can open up your third eye, which can awaken your intuition and increase your awareness and broaden your spiritual horizons. More work can be done in a shorter time frame once you benefit from this framework of being able to live in the present. I feel blessed that the Almighty Creator above us bestowed upon me a life full of challenges and experiences so that I can learn from them and strive to become a better person as I step up my way.

Myth that leads to success: Ignorance is bliss.

Those who think ignorance is bliss are just sloths or dishonest people who refuse to seek the truth in life and prefer to live in complete denial and procrastination. Running away from reality and refusing to live in the present will not solve any problems in your life. Just the opposite, such low-energy thinking will only cause your problems to snowball to the intensity that you will find them even more difficult to resolve as time escalates. The hardest work in life is to put on your thinking cap, so most people shy away from it. Deep thinking can only be achieved through having a sense of consciousness and mindfulness. This is the reason why the most wise and successful men who ever lived spent more time sitting down to think and learn than doing any other activity in their entire life.

COVID-19: With the lockdown, we were all being asked to do social distancing to avoid further spreading of the COVID virus and to be confined in our own living space with minimum physical contact and interaction with the outside world. This inevitably narrows down our scope of communication and gives us more time to be alone to ponder over our lives and plan for what we want to do in our future.

Isolation can also enable us to do some deep thinking and deep work that we might find difficult to do during normal days filled with distractions. Do not mistake living in the present as being complacent and not needing to do any work for our future. Mindfulness brings along creativity and wisdom so that you can understand your inner self in a deeper level and make clear decisive action plans for the future.

CHAPTER 8

The Beauty of Seeking Continuous Improvement

DISCONTENTMENT IS THE seed of change, and someone will never change unless they feel anger or resentment about their current situation. You will never become what you could be until you feel dissatisfied with your current self, which triggers you to seek improvement. Anything that you disapprove or that conflicts with your ethics and principles will cause you to seek change and improvement automatically. Transform things or your current situation by seeking improvement and learning to embrace change rather than resentment. That is why suffering or discomfort are actually great ways for any person to find all ways to seek improvements in their current paradigm. Dare to innovate and seek changes to break through your own comfort zone to bring yourself to the next level. It is so difficult for people to overcome their worry and fear, to step out of the comfort zone to move into a new area of complete uncertainty. A gift is the inherent capacity to fulfill a function that meets a need in creation. No prophecy can give you this gift. From the day you were born, your purpose in life is already given to you. All you need to do in your lifetime is to seek continuous improvement to polish what is already inside you so that you can glorify this gift that is already embedded in you. Education is not about going to school and getting a certificate. A gift can never be learned; it can only be refined. Most people go to school for education potential rather than personal fulfillment. Education is all about constant learning and seeking new knowledge to harness the gift inside you. It has nothing to do with the paper certificates you collect this lifetime that you can showcase in your office or bring along during your job interviews to make you a more favorable candidate. There are so many people who choose a course in their college not because of their personal passion but more from the practical point of attaining a certificate that has a higher commercial value in the realistic working society. No entrepreneur can attain the highest level of success unless they choose a passion that they can eat, sleep, and live with 24-7 and 365 days a year. Only when you are obsessed with your daily profession will this entice your curious mind to seek continuous improvement and acquire relentless knowledge.

Nothing in life is worthwhile unless you take calculated risks. Taking risk involves the courage to embrace changes and, in turn, seek relentless improvement. We have to accept that changes are so rapid in the world we live in, so if we choose to come to a standstill, then blame no one for losing out in this competitive world and being made an outcast. It does not matter when you step into any industry of your chosen field and how far behind you are when you first start the race. What determines the outcome and results are your ability to advance and adapt fast along the journey. Life is never fair, and this is already determined from the day we were born. Unless you are born into a royal or very well-off family (whereby everything in your life will be planned perfectly for you until you go six feet under), I am afraid that you will need to take the life journey like the majority, which will be filled with uncertainty and continuous changes. If we are wise enough to understand and see through this reality from the very beginning, we will be able to better prepare ourselves to adapt with these inevitable adversities.

Reading is one vital habit in life that everyone needs to cultivate in order to ensure a continuous learning process. A lot of great entrepreneurs have daily reading habits and read around fifty to one hundred good books in one calendar year. Reading nonfiction books is my favorite hobby, and wherever I travel, I will always plan ahead and bring along good books to maximize my idle time on the plane or on the road to widen my horizons and gain insight into the mind of all good authors. I try to read from wide categories and try not to narrow down on one specific area. I think the most beneficial kinds of books for entrepreneurs fall into biographies, finance, business, self-help, and enrichment.

In short, if you are not willing to learn to fight for what you think is right by seeking continuous progress and improvement, no one can help you attain success in the entrepreneur path. Expecting your environment to change without yourself transforming is insanity. You must change your daily thought and action in order for your future to change. If you are willing to do whatever it takes to learn consistently no matter what obstacles you have ahead of you, no competitor can stop you from being the first to make it to the top.

After I sold my business and joined the listed group company, I was met with culture shock. Imagine, after my eighteen years of entrepreneurship working independently with absolute freedom and in total control as the sole owner of a small company, now I was working under a corporate umbrella where every single decision, big or small, needs to go through various channels for approval. Such massive changes require a complete switch of mental mindset and psychological adaptation. Throughout this period, I observed how a big organization worked and did a profound comparison of the pros and cons of a small organization versus a big listed group entity. I gained a lot of insight from this exercise. I also did a lot of self-assessment to understand which areas I myself was weak in and sought ways to do self-improvement. The purpose of change is always for the better, so we must always take this from a very open-minded and positive perspective. No system or organization is flawless, so it is often the attitude you exude that determines the outcome of the changes rather than the changes themselves that determine your fate and future.

Myth that lead to success: If things are working well, do not rock the boat; leave things as they are, and don't attempt to change anything.

If everything is running smoothly without any problems or changes, then where do the growth and breakthrough come from? How do you push your limit to the next level if there are no improvements required and everything is in their perfect position? People who had read *Blue Ocean Strategy* understand the difference between the competitive red oceans that are in constant price wars and unhealthy competition versus the blue oceans that thrive based on innovation and thinking out of the box. As an entrepreneur, which ocean would you like to be in? If your choice is the blue ocean, then constant change and adaptation will be the path you will need to choose. Most people do not like changes and will prefer to follow standard protocol to have convenience in life. What most do not realize is that life should never be easy in the first place, which is why humans are the most intelligent species in the animal kingdom. If we are destined to live an easy life, then we will be behaving like other lower animals such as cows, spending six hours each day eating and eight hours chewing cud. Humans are created to use our brains to innovate, revolutionize, and improvise. Happy people are those who find joy in learning and applying what they learn to good use to do good for themselves and for mankind.

COVID-19: This epidemic that has suddenly befallen us mankind left us with not much of a choice but to adapt to the sudden changes to our normal routines and lifestyles.

Some of the changes involve the heavy use of technology for communication when we work from home, the use of online purchases for our basic necessities (which we normally did physically before), and having to work under one roof with our immediate family members, which requires a certain level of tolerance and consideration. During this COVID period, some people will watch more TV, YouTube or Netflix to pass time, and many will turn to more social media platforms to chat and discuss daily happenings, perhaps even circulating and spreading fake news (either intentionally or unintentionally). If we can make use of this COVID lockdown period as a positive change and do more meaningful activities—such as spending more quality time with our family, signing up for online enrichment programs or master classes, completing our wish-list goals that we had no time to work on during normal days, cleaning up our house to eliminate clutter, allocating fixed time to read more, learning new skills that we have passions for, planning out a healthy regimen to exercise daily, and preparing nutritious home-cooked food— we can thereby become better, improved people who have new growth after this lockdown period.

CHAPTER 9

The Beauty of Taking Full Responsibility

PEOPLE'S PATHS ARE all different from the day they were born till the day they die. Entrepreneurs who succeed are always those who bear full responsibility and take control of their own life and destiny. The entrepreneur path is never easy, and along the way, you will inevitably meet with many challenges. Most of these challenges are uncontrollable situations that will put you under immerse pressure and stress. What differentiates great entrepreneurs from others is their ability to stay calm during these situations and to face the storm with fearless courage, taking and accepting full responsibility for whatever the outcome turns out to be.

The problem that most people have is not being able to admit their mistakes whenever things do not turn out as they expect. Truths can be hard to accept, but it is not what happened that determines the quality and quantity of your lives. It is how you face every adverse situation to take full responsibility and find the best way to resolve them that show the true character of a great person. It is often how you react to the situation that determines your fate and destiny. You can only take control of your life if you take full responsibility for your daily actions and thoughts. Everyone likes to take credit, but few like to take the blame. In reality, those who take the blame for what happens in an organization will always be the ones who turn out to be the most successful as their career paths progress. The reason is simple: the law of attraction teaches us that what we reap will be what we sow. How can anyone who shrinks away from their responsibilities be able to take the lead and sit in high positions in any organization? No follower will respect any leader who dares not assume responsibility in times of difficulty.

Our hearts will feel better if we choose to put the blame on our environment or other people for unfortunate things that happen to our lives. When we put ourselves as the victim of a particular situation, we will always feel good hearing about all the comforting words and condolences from people around us. What most people do not realize is that we are actually weakening our ability to resolve problems and become wiser and stronger people by hiding from the truth, blaming other people for any mishaps that happen, or simply blaming our Almighty God as to why such situations happen to us and not to anyone else. It is always during crisis times that opportunity will present itself, and it is during the tough times that you can really differentiate the real leader who stand out from the crowd.

Running away from responsibility is simply an act of cowardice. When we are afraid or fearful of a certain outcome and how it will affect us in a negative fashion, we will tend to shy away from it, just like an ostrich that buries its head in the sand in the sight of danger, without realizing that it is a stupid act that will not resolve the problem. Such acts will only expose your vulnerability to the world and lose you the support and respect of others. Taking full responsibility for your life and helping others around you do the same involves great courage and wisdom that only a handful of people can handle. This is the reason why there is only a small percentage of successful entrepreneurs compared to the mass of working class. To be an entrepreneur means to build something from scratch and to be able to live by it with the oath of being responsible for whatever outcome we make out of it. Without absolute commitment and holding yourself liable for your own business, nothing great will come out from this venture.

Take full responsibility of your life in order to take full control of your life. Take responsibility of where you are in your life, and accept the challenges you face. Do not make excuses or blame others. Focus on what you can. Those who succeed never allow themselves to give or take any excuses. Those who succeed accept all hardships and carry their own baggage through life. Holding on to the excuses and setbacks will only slow you down, so bear full responsibility, learn from it, and move on to continue progressing until you achieve your objective.

My company was set up in year 2002, during the difficult SARS period that lasted for two years and ended in 2004. If I had freaked out and run away from my responsibility, not facing the challenges during this adverse period with courage and integrity, then maybe I would not be writing this book to share my success today. Victory will always follow the leaders who take full responsibility of their own actions. Regardless of whatever era you are in, history itself has already proven that those who are big achievers are always the ones who take ownership of their own decisions and determine their own fate. The challenging SARS period made me fight harder for survival as a new player in our industry. I am grateful for the fact that our company was able to get some of the big distributorships on board during this period, which concretized our foundation and enabled us to build a sound and profitable business. Do not take crises as obstacles, but view them as opportunities. Business personnel will always prefer to work with individuals who possess the great qualities of holding themselves liable and responsible, as they find such attributes reliable, admirable, and trustworthy in business partners.

Myth that leads to success: Safeguard your position in an organization by putting your own interests first so that you will be the last to get the blame.

I have seen lots of such people in my life who will do things for their own interest first rather than thinking of the big picture of the organization. Maybe such acts might work to safeguard their current position, but I do not foresee any future with great advancement. As an organization progresses, the quality of those drivers leading the company also needs to move in parallel. Unless you are happy to always stay put at where you are without any advancement, hiding yourself behind a shield and putting on a mask to face the world will get you nowhere.

COVID-19: Opportunity or woe? This is an interesting question for most entrepreneurs facing the current financial crisis where everything seems to come to a standstill. Some entrepreneurs will use this current situation as an excuse to put blame on their woes and the difficult situation and expecting the government to come to their aid, whereas others who take full responsibility for their own business will try to take control of their own destiny and make the best out of it, doing their very best. After being an entrepreneur for close to two decades, my conclusion is to never expect anyone to fund your business, no matter who they are, be it the banker or the government. The moment you have such a thought, your sense of full responsibility and commitment to what you built will be diluted, and you will lose your absolute power of control. In order to succeed in what you want to build, always leave yourself with no exit route so that you will find all ways for survival and prosperity. This is the basic survival skill that all entrepreneurs should possess.

CHAPTER 10

The Beauty of Good Financial Habits and Financial Literacy

FINALLY, WE REACH the final chapter of my book. No business can succeed without a healthy cash flow and sound finance management. All entrepreneurs who made it to reach financial freedom and build a successful business will go through the process of delayed gratification, a game of leverage versus risk management and capital management.

Focus on abundance and not scarcity if you want to become rich. When I first started my business in the year 2002, all I had was SGD 50,000 of savings in my bank that I managed to accumulate doing two sales jobs simultaneously and working nonstop for sixteen to eighteen hours every single day, including weekends, for a period of fifteen months. To save fifty thousand within a fifteen-month period, having to minus all personal and household expenses as the single breadwinner of a family, requires sound money management and discipline. I did away with all unnecessary expenditures

such as clothing, accessories, eating out, and shopping, and I
would drive all the way to Johor, Malaysia, to buy groceries
and necessities such as formula milk powder and diapers,
since Malaysian Ringgit is weaker than Singapore dollar. If
you are not born rich like me and want to get out of your
rat race so that you can live the rest of your life happily
without having to worry about money should you stop
work tomorrow, then start practicing delayed gratification
and resist the temptation to spend unnecessarily or lavishly
on borrowed money (e.g., overdrafts, lines of credit, credit
cards, and loans of any kind that incur hefty interest rates).
I bought my own first luxury car only ten years later, after
I had already built a strong foundation for my business. The
yearly profit generated from my company for the first ten
years was never spent on any luxury—every dollar spent on
buying properties for passive income investment. We must
fully understand the difference of assets (investments such as
properties and stocks that generate passive positive income)
versus liabilities (your car or the house you stay in that is
rented or still under mortgaged) in order to be financially
sound. Always have the habit to pay yourself first and save up
a certain percentage of your income (at least 20 percent) to
accumulate your first capital, and then invest it wisely to help
you grow and amplify your wealth. The beauty of compound
interest works both ways when you invest early for your own
benefit. And when you take a mortgage loan from a bank
for leverage, know that you need to exercise cautious and
proper care. The hardest thing to achieve is always your first
pot of gold. (For me, that means to earn your first million
dollars.) The magical part is that once you earn the first pot,

the other pots of gold will come by easier and easier, as all you need to do is just cut and paste your successful formula in how you built this first pot of gold to duplicate your wealth fast. I started as a pauper—maybe poorer than the majority of you now reading my book—but never for once did I ever feel deprived. My mind is always thinking of abundance, and I always have this faith that one day, I am going to become rich. I don't think I ever doubted it for a minute from the day I made my first profit, selling erasers to my neighbor for a hefty markup!

Entrepreneurs who make it to the top possess the guts and courage to venture in times of adversity when a majority of people retreat. This is sometimes the business and financial acumen that one will have to naturally equip themselves with upon long-term failure, grinding, self-correction, and continuous improvement. Nothing comes free in life, and do not get me wrong: such natural power acumen can only be acquired if you put in consistent hard work for a long period and transmit this positive energy to the universe in order to receive abundant rewards in return. Sorry for being blunt, but the reality is that during difficult worldwide financial crises, the poor will often become poorer and the rich will get richer. This is the time whereby all branded items such as blue-chip stocks and properties in prime land will be doing their summer or garage sales. Buy them for long-term investment rather than keeping all your money in a safe-haven bank wherein the value will depreciate in time due to inflation and the ever-rising living standard. The inflation rate will always surpass the interest you get from fixed deposits, which is why banks will always have the upper hand similar to when you step into a casino. Your odds and chance of winning will always be smaller than the banker's. Learn the skill of leveraging your hard-earned money to maximize your profit by investing them in the smartest way possible. One main reason many choose the path of entrepreneurship is to build a successful team running a profitable business, which will eventually autopilot to bring in consistent streams of income without the entrepreneur having to work physically anymore. Money cannot buy true happiness, but money *does* give us the option to have convenience and the freedom to choose the kind of lifestyle we want to live. When you are out of the rat race and attain financial freedom, you will also be given the luxury of time to do things you want to fulfill in your life without much worry. It is not the amount you get from your monthly paycheck or income that determines your wealth status. It is your spending habits that define your destiny. I have come across people who earn five-digit salaries and still are in debt due to lavish, extravagant lifestyles. Compare these to people who earn modest salaries but can still become financially independent through prudent lifestyles and good money management. There are basically only two kinds of debts: good debts that you borrow to leverage your financial platform to grow your investment portfolios that generate positive passive income, and bad debts that you borrow to own liabilities that will drown you in deeper financial woes in the long run. By fueling yourself with financial knowledge and backing it up with massive positive actions and discipline, everyone reading this book can achieve this level of success.

Myth that lead to success: Money is the root of all evil, and rich and successful people are selfish and mean.

Money is never the root of any evil, as money is just a tool that has no life by itself. Becoming rich will never make a good soul become evil, nor will it turn an unkind person holy. Having money will only show the true color and integrity of a person. A kind rich person will put money to good use, such as doing philanthropic work, and an unkind person will just use the same money to flaunt their wealth and splurge on material pleasure. Money is a good servant but a bad master. When under absolute discipline and control, money becomes a strong army that can help you fight victorious wars by generating passive income even when you are sleeping. However, if you let greed overcome you, then it becomes your master, and it will brainwash you to act in an unethical fashion that will bring your own downfall. People who can handle big wealth are people of high integrity, for they can withstand the temptation of money, which most of the poor cannot. It all boils down to the wisdom level of a person on whether to use the greenbacks as a useful tool to make our world a better place to live in or to use the same greenback as a harmful tool to destroy mankind.

COVID-19: Through adversity, we usually gain insight and awakening to many things that we normally do not think about. Globally we are now infected by the COVID virus, and even as we are fighting as one united universe to subdue this monster, many nations have had their economies and the livelihood of their commoners all negatively hit. During this challenging period, those who are well planned with their financial literacy, from organizations to individuals, will be able to survive. Those who did not plan for the rainy days will face great difficulties to survive through this period financially. Due to lockdown, many commercial places cannot do business as usual. Tourism, traveling, airlines, transport, construction, and many industries are all badly affected. Many people will lose their jobs, and their household incomes will be an issue. Governments step in to extend their aid by offering tax reduction, cash payouts, and necessities to help their nations tide over this crisis. A person who exercises strict discipline on his financial intelligence will always surpass such economic crises, whereas someone who spends every single dollar in their pocket during the good days will face challenges in this tough time. This real scenario now experienced by mankind should act as a lesson for all to brush up on our financial literacy, to always plan for rainy days that may just hit us without us knowing.

PROFILES OF SUCCESSFUL ENTREPRENEURS

Managing Director Tan Han Leong
Eng Soon Dry Bean Curd Manufacturing Pte. Ltd.

Mr Tan was born into a poor family and grew up in rural Yew Tee Kampong. His father passed away from a traffic accident when he was 13 years old, leaving his mother to bring up 5 children single-handedly.

Like many kids in Singapore during the 1950s, he started working in a bean curd factory at a very young age to help make ends meet. Though young, he was a fast learner and a dedicated worker who quickly mastered every stage of the bean curd making process.

After his employer retired due to old age and had to close the factory in 1977, Mr Tan decided to strike it out on his own at the age of 20 with very little resources. To start his business, he had to borrow $5,000 from his 大舅, Uncle.

To this day, and even though many decades have passed, he remains grateful and appreciative of his Uncle's generosity.

Singaporeans of the Pioneer Generation and Merdeka Generation would know that at that time, basic infrastructure that we take for granted, like water from a tap and piped gas were not common, especially in the *kampongs*. This was post-war Singapore, where the country was still on the road from Third World to First World

To produce his own fried bean curd, also known as *tau pok*, the resourceful and industrious Mr Tan drew water from a nearby well and collected unwanted wasted wood logs to use as fuel to boil the soy milk, process it and finally fry the bean curd to make *tau pok*. He did this over the next 7 years, day after day, overcoming one difficulty after another.

As Singapore matured, so did regulations related to food production. Soon, the government mandated that all food manufacturing activities had to move out from *kampongs* into designated food factories. Enforcement officers went around issuing warnings.

Unfortunately, moving his operations from his backyard into a factory was not possible for Mr Tan at that time. Despite scrimping and saving every cent each month, he simply could not afford factory rentals. And because his family depended on his income, stopping his work suddenly was also not an option.

The authorities came knocking on his door repeatedly and issued fines, which ironically was cheaper than factory rentals. It was not his wish to break the law, but he did so with a heavy heart in order to survive. Each bowl of rice he put on the table for his family was a result of hard work and an iron will.

Together with his family, what kept him going through tough days was his dream of finally being able to afford a factory space of his own, where he could operate freely without the guilt of doing something illegal.

In 1983, this dream became a reality. Mr Tan moved into rented factory and formally registered his company. At age 26, he boldly took a $1 million loan from Hong Leong Finance and brought in an automated bean curd manufacturing line from Japan, being the first in Singapore to do so.

One million dollars is a lot of money today, and it was even larger back then. Some saw it as a huge gamble, but to Mr Tan, he was taking a bold, calculated risk. Indeed, there were problems as soon as the line was up and running. Because the design was from Japan, the bean curd produced was very different from what customers were used to buying and eating, and sales plunged more than 70%.

If things continued this way, Mr Tan would be facing the prospect of bankruptcy. However, with the same hard work, determination and ingenuity that he displayed since the early days of his business, Mr Tan set out to modify the machines himself to produce the desired product, despite not having any education in Engineering.

To this day, this lesson of not expecting things to be smooth sailing just because you have a new technology or hired a capable person is something Mr Tan continues to remind his two sons, who are now involved in helping him run the business.

Mr. Tan's vision of letting both his sons to take over the business had paid off. When they were still young, Mr. Tan would bring them to the factory to learn the ropes and be familiar with his operation. At age five to six, his sons were already "playing" in the packaging department. During school holidays, they would also come to help Mr. Tan manage the daily operation to ensure a smooth ongoing business. Both of his sons are now officially on board to assist Mr. Tan, with one in charge of the morning shift and one in charge of the night shift. (The *tau pok* business is hard work, as the production is fifteen hours per day.) The night shift son needs to start work at 11:00 p.m. to oversee the operation and work throughout the night till next morning. Mr. Tan's conclusion about this arrangement is that letting his sons go to his factory to help out at an early age cultivated their interest and the habit of working hard. Such a challenging role of running a food factory is not a profession that all youngsters are willing to take responsibility of nowadays. It all boils down to Mr. Tan's success in instilling good family discipline and teaching his sons with the right attitude to become successful entrepreneurs.

Words of Wisdom

1. Be a hustler and a hard worker, be persistent, and do not give up easily whatever dreams and ideas you believe in.

2. Have a big vision to see far, and dare to innovate and be different, thus evolving to be the market leader. When others are fearful, be daring. Success goes to those who dare to take calculated risk with well-laid plans.

Eng Soon Dry Beancurd Manufacturing Pte Ltd (Mr Tan Han Leong) with author Moy Teo at homeland Singapore

Managing Director Wang Jinliang
Shandong Kangbeite Food Packaging Machinery Co., Ltd.

Mr. Wang got very basic education and started working at age eighteen as an apprentice in an engineering company in the Shandong province of China during the year 1987. After working for four years, his passion and desire to start his own business spurred him to start a partnership with a friend, Mr. Wang, holding 51 percent of the shareholder stake. After running this business for almost two years, his partner decided to withdraw from this business venture, and Mr. Wang was suddenly faced with financial issues and was in cash-flow difficulty. At the age of twenty-four, Mr. Wang had no choice but to close his company. He went back to the status of working class, this time working as top management in a big corporation doing a similar engineering business.

At age twenty-seven, after sitting in the high position of this big corporation for three years, Mr. Wang understood his calling in life and followed his heart to resign from this high-salary post to pursue his dream of entrepreneurship again, this time as a lone ranger. As he was already married at that time and with a daughter, his decision was greatly objected and opposed by his family. As the path of entrepreneurship involves lots of hard work and uncertainty of income, he faced the pressure of being asked to give up his dream for the sake of giving security to the family. This did not deter his willpower to believe in himself and in what he wanted to achieve in life. He packed his bags and left Shandong Province to venture out with his dream of being a salesman to promote his own innovated creation of packaging machineries to many parts of China.

He suffered a lot of setbacks during his entrepreneurial journey and also got a lot of rejections. He did not give up hope and continued his hustling while seeking ways to improve his creation. All negative comments and feedback by his potential customers were taken on board in a very positive manner. He literally got a China associate to help him get hold of a German competitor brand and physically dismantled the whole machine to study and analyze every single part to benchmark against his own invention. In return, he offered to service this German machine free of charge to reciprocate the kindness of this friend. When he shared this story with me, I could not help but think of Henry Ford, founder of the Ford automobile company, who developed and manufactured the first automobile that many middle class people could afford after he improved the production time of one Ford car from twelve hours to two hours and thirty minutes.

Kangbeite is now a renowned brand within Mainland China for supplying premium-quality packaging machines at affordable prices. Mr. Wang expresses his gratitude to all his customers who have supported him along the way in this challenging entrepreneur path. He mentioned special thanks to Mr. Wong Chee Meng, business owner of Full Glory Sdn. Bhd. (Malaysia), for being a friend–cum–mentor who helped him and guided him along in his time of need. He also stuck to his principle to stand out from the rest of the local-made China brand competitors by adhering to producing high-quality machineries and not using inferior materials to maximize the profit. Nothing beats trust in life, so never tarnish your reputation by trying to undercut your quality.

Shandong Province, in the state of Lu, is well-known for their culture of religion and Taoist influence, with Qufu being the birthplace of the great wise Confucius. Shandong people are also well-known for their sense of righteousness, frankness, warmth, and hospitality. It was a great honor to know Mr. Wang and to have him share his beautiful story of entrepreneurship.

Words of Wisdom

1. Build positive social circles that help you along the way, even in times of adversity, and always apply humility and gratitude in life.
2. Live with integrity, and produce products that you yourself are satisfied with in terms of quality and standard. Never compromise quality for monetary gains.

Shandong Kangbeite Food Packaging Machinery Co Ltd
Mr Wang Jinliang at PWTC exhibition in Kuala
Lumpur, Malaysia with Moy Teo (July year 2018)

Managing Director Mr. Lee Lee Kong
Ayam Wira Food Processing Sdn bhd

At age sixty-nine, Mr. Lee is still waking up early in the morning, driving by himself to visit his farms or going to one of his companies to oversee daily operation matters. He is now acting like a consultant, guiding his three sons who had taken over his business—from hatchery farm to slaughterhouse and halal processed meat plant making value-added products such as burgers, nuggets, and sausages.

During the year 1961, at a mere age of ten, Mr. Lee had to wake up 5:00 a.m. every morning to go to the wet market and help his father slaughter chickens. He would then change to his school uniform and go for his class at 11:00 a.m. This lasted for three years, and at age thirteen, Mr. Lee was asked to stop schooling due to poor family environment—his father could no longer afford to support him to do so anymore. Mr. Lee quit school and helped out at his father's wet market stall for ten years to make ends meet. At age twenty-three, he got married, and his father set up a mini market for his wife to run a small business when he turned twenty-four.

His career took a turning point when he turned twenty-six, when he could not see eye-to-eye with his elder brother, who was also helping in his father's small business. He came out to set up his first trading company, getting chicken carcasses from a factory, and he started selling wholesale in the state of Klang. He was basically a one-man show, employing only one worker to help him with the manual delivery while he ran the sales and did his own delivery using his father's truck.

His business acumen and great salesmanship accelerated the revenue of his trading company at a speedy rate, and after grinding for three years, he became a renowned top salesman in the state of Klang. As all his competitors were based in the state of Kuala Lumpur, he had the advantage of geographical location, since he could save on transport expenses in not having to truck from Kuala Lumpur to Klang.

A big challenge knocked on his door after three years of conquering the market share for the state of Klang. A big corporation realized his presence posed a threat for their business and started to create a price war to compete with him in a red ocean strategy battle. Knowing that this was the critical period of his entrepreneurship, Mr. Lee's foresight led him to set up his own agriculture farming at age thirty, loaning a big sum of money from the bank and risking it all to either perish or survive. He was fully aware that unless he could own his source of chickens, he would never be able to outwit this competition. At age thirty-two, Mr. Lee continued to expand his ambition to cement his position in the industry by setting up his own slaughterhouse. With this slaughterhouse, he was able to process all the chickens from his own farm and portion all the cuts to sell to his clients based on their requirements. He also built a lot of cold rooms and freezers, and he invested in IQF technology, as with that he could store his carcasses for longer periods and sell to the market when prices were up. Once again, his foresight and guts enabled him to move up to the next level of his entrepreneurship.

At age thirty-five, Mr. Lee set up his own hatchery farm, investing in the latest technology to breed their own chickens rather than buying baby chicks for farming. At age forty-six, Mr. Lee fulfilled his dream of building the top-line-to-bottom-line concept by setting up his own value-added factory producing nuggets, burgers, and sausages using his own raw materials from his farm and slaughterhouse.

Mr. Lee enjoys travelling and still flies extensively to different parts of the world up till today to see the latest innovation machineries and finished products, and bring back those ideas to share with his sons to explore ways of bringing their family-owned business to the next level.

All of us younger or soon-to-be entrepreneurs need to learn from the spirit of Mr. Lee for having a curious and open mind, seeking continuous improvement, and applying flexibility and adapting new ideas and concepts regardless of age.

Words of Wisdom

1. Never do a trade that you are not familiar with. Be totally hands on, focused, and put in all your hard work to be the master of your game before you pass to your team players to run the show.
2. Integrity and reputation are the most important principles for business, and abstain from bad habits such as gambling.

Ayam Wira Food Processing Sdn Bhd
Mr Lee Lee Kong at Zhucheng Dinosaur National Geopark
in Shandong China (2nd from right), Mr Guan Yan
Cong- Shandong Zhonghanghuijin Composite Materials
Technology co, Ltd (Extreme Left), Mr Wang Jinliang
Shandong Kangbeite Food Packaging Machinery Co, Ltd.
(Extreme Right) with author Moy Teo (2nd from Left)

Lightning Source UK Ltd.
Milton Keynes UK
UKHW012257220520
363742UK00008B/337